Philosophy in the
West Indian Novel

Philosophy in the West Indian Novel

Earl McKenzie

University of the West Indies Press
Jamaica • Barbados • Trinidad and Tobago

University of the West Indies Press
7A Gibraltar Hall Road   Mona
Kingston 7   Jamaica
www.uwipress.com

13 12 11 10 09   5 4 3 2 1

McKenzie, Earl.
Philosophy in the West Indian novel / Earl McKenzie.
p. cm.
Includes bibliographical references.
ISBN: 978-976-640-215-0
1. West Indian fiction (English) – History and criticism. 2. Philosophy in literature.
I. Title.

PR9214.M34 2009   823.09

Cover illustration: Detail from *Calabash Totem* (2007) by Earl McKenzie.

Book and cover design by Robert Kwak.
Set in Caslon.

Printed in the United States of America.

To Dorothy Robertson, my first teacher of literature.

Contents

Preface

This book is the result of one philosopher's response to ten West Indian novels. It is based on three main assumptions. First, that philosophy is reflection on the deepest questions we can ask about ourselves and our world. Second, that literature, and especially the novel, is the best method yet devised to give "a human face" to those reflections. And third, that the philosophical study of Caribbean literature can contribute something of value to the development of Caribbean academic philosophy.

There are many conceptions of philosophy, and I believe that debate on this question should be an important part of the process of trying to develop philosophy in the region. In any philosophical venture, I think it helps to be clear about the conception of the discipline within which one is working. I believe that philosophy is a natural human activity and that philosophical questions although universal, may be modified by their historical and social contexts. I am not what in some circles would be called a culturalist: someone who believes that philosophical questions are deeply embedded in particular cultures, and that they can be understood only in these contexts. I believe that philosophical reflection has always been a part of West Indian life, even if it has not been well documented and is at the present time relatively undeveloped and unsystematized. There are important historical and sociological questions as to why academic philosophy has not yet emerged as an important part of West Indian intellectual life. These questions may have something to do with certain facts of the region's history – slavery, colonialism, imperialism, and so on – or with certain patterns of historical development according to which the more reflective and analytical aspects of culture tend to come later. These are questions which persons interested in the development of Caribbean philosophy should explore.

The relationship between philosophy and literature is ancient. There are cultures in which the two are virtually indistinguishable. The connection which interests me most here is that of philosophy in the novel: the view that novels can embody philosophical ideas in the form of human life, and thereby make them not only more accessible to readers, but provide what is arguably the best way of testing their truth or plausibility. I do not take what Nussbaum somewhere calls a hedonistic approach to literature. While I agree that aesthetic pleasure is one of the values of literature, and one which can aid its other values, my main view here is of philosophy and literature as allies in the exploration of questions which seem to me to be of enormous importance. Of course, philosophy is by no means the only discipline which may see literature as an ally. Marx once said that there is more sociology in the nineteenth-century English novel than in the textbooks. Psychologists, theologians and historians are only some of the other scholars who may be inclined to make appeals to literature.

West Indian philosophizing, I submit, is at the present time mostly embedded in other forms of cultural expression like literature, religion, political institutions, and so on. Excavating what is already there is therefore an important preliminary task in the process of developing a more self-aware and reflective philosophical awareness. This book is an attempt at doing this with respect to literature.

I wish to thank Professor Earl Winkler of the University of British Columbia who introduced me to the area of philosophy in literature. Thanks are also due to the Research Fellowship Programme of the University of the West Indies, Mona, for the fellowship which made the research possible. I thank my students here at Mona, especially those in my course on philosophy in literature, whose sharp and eager questions made me feel the need for a book of this kind. I also wish to thank Dr Nadi Edwards and Roxanne Burton for library assistance. Special thanks to Karleen Morgan and Verdine Stephenson for their typing services and patience and endurance in dealing with my idiosyncrasies.

Introduction

In the Western tradition, the relation between philosophy and literature has a long lineage. As Rickman (1996) reminds us, some of philosophy's most famous ideas have been communicated through literary images: Plato's allegory of the cave as a representation of the human condition; Kant's image of the flying dove complaining about the air's resistance to its wings as an illustration of the importance of sense experience; and Hegel's use of the imagery of the owl which flies at dusk as a symbolization of philosophy's retrospective view of history. It is well known that philosophers have long used a variety of literary forms to embody their ideas. Famous examples include Plato's *The Symposium*, Nietzsche's *Thus Spake Zarathustra*, Voltaire's *Candide*, and Sartre's novels and plays. In addition, many writers not normally considered philosophers, for example, Tolstoy, Dostoevsky, Shakespeare and Eliot, have created works of considerable philosophical importance. Philosophers, writers and readers know that one of the best ways of testing the truth or plausibility of a philosophical idea, is to embody it in the form of human life, and literature, especially the novel, is arguably the best method yet devised for doing so.

Philosophy and literature intersect in many ways, so it is necessary to be clear about the connection being explored here, so it is not confused with others.

This is not a work on *philosophy as literature*. Such a field exists, as some of the great philosophers, like Plato and Nietzsche, were also gifted writers, and many of their works can be studied as literature. I am not aware that the Caribbean has yet produced any works of this kind, but it may do so in the future.

Neither is this a book on the *philosophy of literature*. Every discipline has a philosophical dimension, and this includes literature. Philosophy of literature studies the conceptual, logical and normative foundations of literature as a discipline, and so much of what it does is close to what is now called literary theory. A book on the philosophy of the West Indian novel would be subsumed under this branch of philosophy. While I think such a book could be written, and would be an interesting project, this work is something different.

This book is not an exercise in *philosophy through literature*. Teachers of philosophy have long recognized that philosophical problems often appear, in a preliminary form, in virtually every genre of literature: novels, short stories, plays, poems, fables, myths, parables, and so on. Since they know that students usually find it easier to relate to the characters and situations in such works than to abstract philosophical questions and arguments, they use these works as starting points for their investigations. In these cases the major emphasis is on the post-literary explorations. While a philosophy teacher could use this book in this way, by using West Indian characters and situations as starting points for philosophical inquiry, the book is not structured to go all the way in this kind of investigation.

This is a work of *philosophy in literature*. Like real people, literary characters encounter philosophical problems, and must find ways of making sense of them. Some famous examples will illustrate what I mean. In the Bible, Job encounters the problem of evil, and a mystical experience gives him a way of dealing with it. In Greek drama, Oedipus wrestles with the problem of free will versus fatalism, and chooses to accept responsibility for his actions by inflicting punishment on himself. When writers create literary characters who engage with philosophical questions or have experiences which give rise to such questions, and the writers employ effective literary and aesthetic strategies to dramatize this aspect of human experience, then we have philosophy in literature. This book examines some West Indian examples of this.

Given the paucity of academic philosophy in the West Indian intellectual tradition, any book with the words "philosophy" and "West Indian" in its title is likely to arouse some curiosity, even suspicion, as to its contents. Space does not allow for much consideration of the contentious question of how to define exactly what philosophy is. Anyone familiar with the discipline will understand why the nature of philosophy, like that of science, religion, art, or any other discipline, is itself a very demanding philosophical issue; philosophers call this kind of self-reflection "metaphilosophy". The only metaphilosophical position relevant here is that, for the purposes of this book, I regard philosophy as a discipline which deals with questions of a certain kind which students of the subject learn to spot when they encounter them, and to develop strategies for dealing with them. Examples of these questions are: What should the aims of education be? (chapter 1); What is the meaning of life? (chapter 2); What is the self? (chapter 3). Each chapter of the book examines at least one such question in a West Indian context.

It is also important to note the relation between philosophy and literary theory. Rickman (1996) sees them as rivals. He argues that literary theory has grown to fill a gap caused by the relative underdevelopment of the philosophy of literature, which, unlike similar disciplines – the philosophy of science, for instance – has not flourished. Rickman sees literary theory as an attempt to create a superdiscipline which arises out of other disciplines such as philosophy, psychology and sociology. Certainly, literary theory draws on the two dominant philosophical cultures in the world today: Anglo-American analytic philosophy and Continental philosophy. Its emphasis on performative uses of language, for example, clearly comes from speech act theory in the analytic tradition, especially in the work of the British philosopher J.L. Austin. Its debt to the Continental tradition includes the contribution of Jacques Derrida, a French philosopher who developed the theory known as deconstruction; the work of Michel Foucault, another French philosopher, who developed discourse theory, and the influence of phenomenology, especially as developed by the Austrian philosopher Edmund Husserl, on many aspects of literary studies – reader-response criticism among them. The influence of philosophy on literary theory has also spread to its offshoot, cultural studies. I am aware of some of the issues in literary theory, as well as some of the tensions with philosophy. That awareness forms a backdrop to my interpretation of the novels, but this is not a work of literary theory.

Neither is it, essentially, a work of literary criticism, although there will be an obvious awareness of this practice's philosophical rootedness in literary theory as well as in aesthetics and the philosophy of art. Sometimes my background in literary criticism will be evident. There is very little of what Culler (1997, 61–62) calls poetics: the study of how literary works achieve their meanings. But there is a good deal of what he calls hermeneutics: the process of interpreting and giving meanings to literary works. I shall not claim that the meanings I attribute to these works are those intended by their authors. My position on this contentious matter is that a work is open to all the interpretations which it can logically bear. My inclination towards reader-response criticism will be evident in what follows.

This book is intended as a contribution to Caribbean philosophy. So far, academic philosophy has not flourished in the West Indies. But it seems to be taking off. The subject is gaining in popularity here at the Mona campus of the University of the West Indies, and there are initiatives underway at the other campuses. The Caribbean Philosophical Association is about to be formed. Books and articles have been appearing, or are in the making.

It is my view that the philosophical study of West Indian literature has an important role to play in the emergence of Caribbean philosophy. I think that at our present stage, Caribbean philosophical thought is mostly embedded in other forms of cultural expression like literature, religion, and politics. The first task facing us, therefore, is to excavate what is there. These are the foundations on which the future edifice of Caribbean philosophy may hopefully be built.

I was trained in analytic philosophy and this, for the most part, will be the vantage point from which my chosen texts will be approached. But I am very wary of restricting myself with labels. I have considerable respect for the Continental tradition's seemingly greater willingness to engage with a wider variety of disciplines, and thereby avoid the narrow scientism of which analytic philosophy is sometimes accused. I also think that Caribbean philosophy can learn a lot from the Continental tradition's emphasis on the critique of social praxis aimed at social emancipation (Critchley 2001, 54–74). More importantly, especially for this book, is the fact that I have a strong interest in world philosophies. I take seriously Lamming's view that "a whole planet collapsed in this Archipelago: Europe, Africa, Asia and the ancient ecology of a diverse Amerindian ancestry" (Lamming 1999, vii). I will therefore draw on several of our peoples' ancestral philosophies, especially European philosophy and its offshoots, African philosophy and Indian philosophy.

The novels I examine were selected to reflect differences in geography, chronology, ethnicity and gender. My aim is to examine the West Indian novel as an imaginative dramatization of the philosophical ideas, assumptions and presuppositions which undergird lived experience in the Caribbean. I shall try to show that these novels raise questions which lie at the philosophical heartland of our West Indian way of life.

Chapter 1

Aims of Education
Historicism and *In the Castle of My Skin*

What should the aims of education be? This question is one of the central issues in the philosophy of education. In the Caribbean context this question may be divided into two: What were the aims of colonial education? and What should be the aims of postcolonial education? In this chapter I wish to argue that in his novel *In the Castle of My Skin* ([1953] 1987) Lamming presents some of the answers to the first question. The conclusion of the novel raises the second.

Linked with the protagonist's educational experiences, but also recurring outside of them, is the issue of historicism. Henry (2000) contends that historicism is one of the dominant tendencies in Afro-Caribbean philosophy. I wish to argue that this tendency is also evident in Lamming's novel. But I shall deal with the aims of colonial education first, and then take up the issue of historicism.

In the novel we follow G, the protagonist, from experiences in the village school to experiences in the high school. He is one of only a handful of boys who, on the basis of their performance in the public examinations, are promoted to the high school. These two schools exist in separate worlds and serve different social classes, and the fact that G moves from one to the other creates difficulties for him. My strategy here will be to infer the aims of colonial education from the phenomenology of education in these types of schools which Lamming describes.

I begin with the village school. It is Empire Day. The aim is to use spectacle to impress the boys with the greatness of the British Empire. About one thousand boys form nine squads in a formation which, seen from the porch, resembles a slave ship. The school is decorated with an abundance of red, white and blue flags of varying shapes and sizes bearing images of princes and kings, thrones, ships and empires. The school inspector, a white Englishman, arrives in his car. There is a flag on its bonnet and he is also wearing the three colours. Regarding the effect of the spectacle Lamming writes: "In every corner of the school the tricolour Union Jack flew its message. The colours though three in number had by constant repetition produced something vast and terrible, a kind of pressure or presence of which everyone was a part" (Lamming 1987, 28). Apparently, this use of spectacle to impress colonial subjects began in Victoria's reign (Booker and Juraga 2001, 38).

Moral suasion is one of the ways of securing allegiance to a cause or institution. It is one of the devices used by the inspector as he tries to earn the boys' loyalty to the British Empire by convincing them that it rests on laudable moral foundations, and that its goals are morally admirable. With such moral goals, he wants to say, who could be against it? He says: "The British Empire, you must remember, has always worked for the peace of the world. This was the job assigned it by God, and if the Empire at any time has failed to bring about that peace it was due to events and causes beyond its control" (Lamming 1987, 30). God and religion are often used to back up moral claims, and this is what the inspector does. In short, if you are against the Empire you are against the promotion of peace in the world. You are also against the will of God.

Another aim of colonial education was to shape behaviour into the desired submissive forms through the use of drills, regimentation and force.

According to Lamming, the head teacher "blew the whistle and there was complete silence. He blew it again and they all sat. They knew the rules. They were trained. Each pipe of the whistle meant something, and they knew that something. They were well trained" (pp. 66–67). When school is dismissed the boys march out of the building, with military precision, to the accompaniment of the school song. The use of violence is part of this regimentation. All the teachers carry canes as if they are afraid of being attacked by the boys. And they use the canes frequently. The head teacher brutally beats a boy who begins to speak while the teacher is trying to find out which student has laughed at a mention of the queen. It is later revealed that it was Boy Blue who had asked if "the queen's bloomers was red white and blue" (p. 36). It turns out that the victim's mother is the head teacher's servant and she knows what goes on in his house.

The head teacher is an agent of the Empire. Normally a serious man, he smiles throughout the duration of the inspector's visit. The inspector too, "smiled all the time, while the head teacher grinned jovially as if he and the inspector were part of a secret the others were to guess" (p. 30). The secret, of course, is that they are united in the task of carrying out the Empire's will. This is explicitly stated in the following observation: "They made a striking contrast in appearance, but they seemed in a way to belong to the same thing" (p. 31). Even when they seem to be speaking man to man they are really playing a cat-and-mouse game with the inspector as the cat.

But the head teacher, as a man with education – a rare commodity then – is an important person in the village. Villagers seek his advice on virtually everything: "Marriage, religion, sin, work" (p. 59). He reads the lesson at church and sometimes buries the dead. He is a poor village boy who has made something of himself. An important agent of socialization, he advises the boys not to shout in the streets, to be careful when crossing the road, and to be polite to their elders.

In addition to the idea that the Empire is morally praiseworthy, there is a desire to portray its benevolence. This is done by giving the boys pennies on Empire Day. Depending on their standard, some of the boys get one penny, others two; Exhibitioners get three. The pennies are a gift from the queen. The students are fascinated by the manufacture of the coins, and the head teacher advises them to spend their gifts wisely. But the inspector never stays for the distribution of the pennies. Is he perhaps embarrassed by this blatant buying of loyalty?

As for its curriculum, the village school aims only at teaching the basics. Trumper, one of G's friends who has recently returned from the United States, claims that apart from teaching him how to write his name and count, the school taught him nothing that was of use in later life. On Empire Day the students' performance for the inspector – they are competing for a shield and have practised for the past three months – consists of a nonsense rhyme, a hurricane jingle and one stanza of a hymn. (Perhaps a jingle telling them when to expect hurricanes is useful in the tropics!) The hymn reminds them that a large church (three times the size of the school building) is situated on the same compound, and it underscores the school's affiliation with the Anglican Church. (Religion is one of the novel's main themes but we will explore it no further here.) Yet the head teacher, in referring to the three exhibitioners who have qualified for the high school, claims he is proud of the good foundation – especially in mathematics – that his school has given them.

According to Lamming "the village school served the needs of the villagers, who were poor, simple and without a very marked sense of social prestige" (pp. 210–11). Most graduates of this school start learning a trade after they leave; they become carpenters and shoemakers; some, like G's friend, become policemen; the academically gifted ones become pupil teachers at the school and perpetuate the elementary school system which has remained relatively unchanged over the years.

Angered by their misbehaviour, the head teacher tells the boys that he expects students from Groddeck's Boy School to be gentlemen. "Gentlemen," he says, "don't grin and giggle like buffoons, and in the presence of respectable people, people of power and authority" (pp. 34–35). To be a gentleman, in his view, is to show deference to power and authority. There are, of course, important distinctions between power and authority. Each can exist without the other, even if, ideally they should go together. Though respect for legitimate authority may be part of what it means to be a gentleman, I do not think submitting to power is part of the meaning of the word. But submission to British power and "authority" is one of the aims of British colonial education. The English gentleman is virtually an archetype of British culture – I shall say more about this later.

Another aim of British colonial education was the replication of Britain's educational institutions in the colonies. During Empire Day there is loud applause, when the inspector says "such a display as I have seen here could not have been bettered by the lads at home" (p. 30). After the applause, the head teacher shakes the inspector's hand "gratefully" and leads a cheer for the school.

Fanon (1963, 216) observes that colonialism aims at the distortion, disfigurement and destruction of the history of the colonized. This is evident in the novel. The boys overhear the older folk talking about Queen Victoria who, it is said, freed them. The boys try to make sense of this notion. An old woman says they were once slaves, and that it was the queen who had freed them. They ask a teacher to explain the meaning of "slave". This is the response: "And moreover it had nothing to do with people in Barbados. No one there was ever a slave, the teacher said. It was in another part of the world that those things happened. Not in Little England" (Lamming 1987, 49). The fact that slavery was a major part of Barbadian history – and that there were slave insurrections – is completely denied. They are taught that slavery was in the distant past: "They had read about the Battle of Hastings and William the Conqueror. That happened so many hundred years ago. And slavery was thousands of years before that. It was too far back for anyone to worry about teaching it as history. That's really why it wasn't taught. It was too far back. History had to begin somewhere, but not so far back" (Lamming 1987, 50). The boys are taught to take pride in the fact that Barbados is "the oldest and least adulterated of British colonies" (p. 17).

Yet in spite of attempts at deceiving them, we get the impression that not all the boys are fooled. Anticipating Bob Marley's "mental slavery" idea, one of the boys says: "The old woman isn't an old fool. She knew what she was saying. She was a slave. We're all slaves. The queen freed some of us, but most of us are still slaves" (p. 62).

At age eleven, two years older than he was at the start of the novel, G enters the high school. The promotion turns him away from his friends, Frumpy, Bob and Boy Blue, and begins a process of alienation from his village culture and roots. But he is joyous that his mother's support and the private lessons have paid off and he enters the school "alert and energetic" (p. 209).

The high school is a kinder, gentler place than the village school. G finds the surroundings exciting. There is an orchard and a cricket pitch. There is dialogue between the boys and the masters – even if it is often facetious on the part of the boys. There are fewer restrictions and the boys seem happier. There is no inspector or supervising minister, but the governor and bishop are usually invited to prize-giving functions. The aim of the high school is "to educate the children of the clerical and professional classes" (p. 210). Its graduates enter the civil service or go to English universities to be trained in professions like law and medicine; its failures migrate to the United States.

The two schools reflect the class divisions in the society. G finds it difficult to reconcile the two worlds: "It was as though my roots had been snapped from the centre of which I knew best, while I remained impotent to wrest what my fortunes had forced me into" (p. 212). The people in his village, where he continues to live, now regard him as belonging to the other side. He regards the two schools as a steeplechase with the contestants jumping over different hurdles which lead in different directions and which never meet.

During his six years at the high school, G sees himself alternating between "boyish indifference and tolerable misery" (p. 217). The school "seemed a ship with a drunk crew" (p. 210). At the brink of expulsion, the headmaster tells him that it is the aim of the school to produce gentlemen, and that it seems as if G does not belong. Unlike the head teacher at the village school, the headmaster does not spell out what he means by the term. The behaviour of the "English Gentleman" is governed by a strict code often portrayed (sometimes satirically) in novels and films. The point that Lamming wants to make, it seems, is that G fails to be a satisfactory product of the ultimate aim of a colonial education for boys. He is rescued when, as an alternative to expulsion, he is turned over to the first assistant who directs his reading and gives him access to his personal library. This relationship, he says, is the only part of high school for which he feels grateful.

The main historical experience at the high school occurs after the outbreak of World War II when militarism becomes a part of the school curriculum. The boys are drilled and trained in the use of Bren and Sten guns. According to the narrator, "This war wasn't history. It was real . . ." (p. 214).

G has managed to acquire some competence in two foreign languages. As he is about to leave the high school, he gets a job in Trinidad to teach English to South Americans. A product of a colonial education, he is, himself, about to become an educator. It can be argued that the colonial masters had a clearer view of their aims of education than do their postcolonial successors. But we are left to wonder what G's goals as an educator will be. We are given his critique of colonial education, but what will he, and others like him, put in its place? As he is about to embark on his teaching career he tells us: "I promised that I would start afresh, a new man among other men" (p. 219).

Apart from being a facet of the educational experiences of the protagonist, historicism is, I submit, a dominant theme of the novel. By historicism, I mean any emphasis of historical development in an attempt at understanding the world. It is any awareness of the historicity of the human condition, of the fact that our thoughts and actions, and even our acts of imagination are, to a very large extent, shaped by history. It is the study not only of the past but of our ways of thinking about the past. Historicism has not been a dominant trend in recent Anglo-American philosophy, but I agree with Margolis (2000) that it will return. The novel is also a meditation on history. Lamming is true to Fanon's dictum that in colonial societies men of culture should "take their stand in the field of history" (Fanon 1963, 209).

In the novel we see the boys – G and his friend – trying to make historical sense of living in Barbados. They have read, or heard, of great persons in European history, but as Hegel put it, infamously, they feel as if they are outside of history, or if somehow history has nothing to do with them. So they are determined to make history. While they are at the pipe cleaning up the boy who defecated while he was beaten by the head teacher, they talk about taking revenge on the teacher.

> Third Boy: In a matter like this we won't have no supporters at all. We'll be making hist'ry if we stone him.
> Fourth Boy: We going to make hist'ry. I always want to make some hist'ry.
> Second Boy: Me too. I read, 'bout all those who been making hist'ry, William the Conqueror an Richard an all these. I read how they make hist'ry, an I say to myself, 'tis time I make some too.
> First Boy: We going to make hist'ry, by Foster Fence. Let's make hist'ry. (Lamming 1987, 40)

They decide against stoning the head teacher, but the idea occurs to them that they too can do extraordinary things and make history.

While on the beach the boys recount some of the oral history of their village – like the story of Bots, Bambina and Bambi. Boy Blue observes that although many things happen in their village, history has not taken note of them. He says, "Those things never happen in hist'ry, an' even if they did, hist'ry ain't got eyes to see everything" (p. 133).

During their crab hunt, the boys are curious about the history of Barbados, and other places they have heard about, like America and England.

> "But what about America?" Trumper asked.
> "America?" Bob got up from the rocks.

> "You talking about the olden times," he said, "You talkin' about a way back
> in 1492. But Barbados was discovered by the English in 16 something or
> the other, an' that is modern times."
> "An' who discovered America?" Trumper asked.
> "The English too," Bob said quickly.
> "An' where the English come from?" Boy Blue asked.
> "From England," Bob said, making the question seem ridiculously simple.
> (p. 148)

We see the kind of regressing queries so common among children. The boys are trying to sort out and make sense of such historical data as have been conveyed to them. One of them regurgitates what has obviously been inculcated in him: "Bob smiled and to our utter astonishment spoke with a kind of religious conviction: 'Barbados or Little England, an island of coral formation set like a jewel in the Caribbean Sea' " (p. 148). The "Little England" mythology has long been, and continues to be, a central part of Barbadian lore.

The boys also apply their history lessons to their experience. Their being on the beach brings back the story of King Canute. According to the story – which is not retold in the novel – King Canute, in order to convince his subjects that he was not a god, had himself taken to the beach where he unsuccessfully commanded the waves to come no further. With much pleasure, the boys re-enact Canute's unsuccessful commanding of the waves. But the story also raises a question about the reality of history:

> "Who king is this?" Boy Blue asked.
> "Canute," said Trumper. "King Canute".
> "Where he come from?" asked Boy Blue.
> Bob and Trumper laughed. "He's the king in the hist'ry book" said
> Trumper.
> "But where he live?" asked Boy Blue.
> "He don't live," said Trumper, getting angry. "It's hist'ry." (p. 111)

They have not been taught to regard history as a living reality. They do not know what to make of the King Canute story: is it a story, a joke or serious business? They re-enact it but fail to draw its religious conclusion, that man does not have God-like powers.

The shoemaker is one of the most historically significant characters in the novel. " 'Things change an' times too,' said the shoemaker; ''tis all in history' " (p. 95). He has read about the Greeks, Alexander the Great, the Roman Empire, the Spanish Empire, the Portuguese Empire and the British Empire of which Barbados is a part. But even the British Empire will change too, he argues. God will destroy it when it starts to get ugly.

He complains that they were never taught about Marcus Garvey, their brother, who he mistakenly thinks lives in Africa. "'Tain't no joke,' the shoemaker said; 'if you tell half of them that work in those places they have somethin' to do with Africa they'd piss straight in your face'" (p. 96). His shop is a meeting place where he discusses history and current events with the villagers.

Significantly, he is one of the first victims of historical change in the village. Through the machinations of Mr Slime, the teacher turned politician and businessman, who is the new landowner in the village, the land on which the shoemaker has lived for twenty years is sold, and the building is destroyed when they try to move it.

Ma and Pa are the two oldest inhabitants of the village and they are the repositories of an oral tradition and the wisdom of the ages. While things are changing around them, Pa has a dream and talks in his sleep. He talks about Africa: "One question remain which we answer by quiet: wherefore was Africa and the wildness around it and the darkness above and beyond the big sea?" (p. 202). He remembers the tribes and their numerous gods. He also remembers the selling of slaves, the selling of the best of Africa. This "ancient silver" is the cause of the sickness of the islands. He makes his peace with the Middle Passage. He recognizes the difficulty of any "back to Africa" movement. He claims that Columbus's mistake is the only certainty inherited by islanders, including Slime and Creighton. He does not know the fate of the islands, but he knows that a man must choose to live like a god or a dog.

Pa is also a victim of historical change in the village. After Ma's death his house is sold – the head teacher wants to buy it – and at the end of the novel he is about to be taken to the Alms House. Pa, too, is a victim of Mr Slime's ascendancy.

The novel is mostly about the march of history – as Hegel would put it – through Creighton Village and, by extension, Barbados, over a period of approximately nine years. It is a fictional autobiography said to be based largely on Lamming's own life – a *bildungsroman* chronicling aspects of G's childhood and adolescence from his ninth birthday to the eve of his departure for Trinidad. But it is also an account of the transformation of a village. When the novel begins we find what is virtually a semi-feudal village. The land is owned by Creighton, a white man who lives on a hill, with the villagers being his tenants. Then there are the labour riots in which Creighton is nearly killed. These usher in the nationalist movement. Mr Slime is a big figure in this transformation. A former teacher at the village school, he resigns and forms a Penny Bond and Friendly Society, and the villagers are encouraged to save their money in these institutions with a view to eventually buying the land on which they live. But Mr Slime, who is appropriately named, uses this money – and his education – to gain wealth and power, and when the novel ends, he is on his way to succeeding Creighton as the owner of the village.

From what Cooke (1990) calls the apocalyptic flood which destroys G's birthday party at the start of the novel, to the racial consciousness which Trumper brings back from the United States, the novel chronicles the consciousness, and social context, of a young man who, according to Gikandi, is unable to "inherit his history and cultural tradition" (Booker and Juraga 2001, 27). The novel is a call for an alternative history, and for an educational philosophy which will accommodate and promote this history. Published thirteen years before Barbados achieved its independence from Britain, this call is still relevant to our times.

Chapter 2

The Meaning of Life and *Black Lightning*

The climactic event in *Black Lightning* ([1955] 1983) is the suicide of Jake, the protagonist. Suicide may sometimes be seen as the ultimate consequence of a lack of meaning in one's life. The search for this meaning and the ethics of suicide are important philosophical issues. I will try to show that in *Black Lightning* these issues are closely related. In my interpretation, the novel shows how the absence of meaning in his life can drive a good man to the irrationality and immorality of suicide.

In describing the circumstances that lead to Jake's suicide, Mais, by implication, points out factors which could have made his life meaningful. But Jake fails to find meaning, and he confronts what Camus (1955, 11) sees as the fundamental question of philosophy: Is life worth living? Jake answers that question negatively with his suicide.

A meaningful life often includes the following: (1) religion; (2) a positive view of suffering; (3) loving relationships with others; (4) a vocation, and (5) moral conduct (Hanfling 1987). Mais's portrait of Jake suggests that his suicide is a result of his failure to have these elements in his life. I shall consider each of them in turn.

Many would argue that the chief function of religion is to give life meaning. Through religion, people seek some cosmic purpose for their lives, connection with a larger, usually transcendent being, or contact with the sacred within themselves.

We are told that Jake "was not a deeply religious man, just about average for those parts. That is to say he went to church about one Sunday in every month, paid his dues and the other days conducted himself in a normal civilized way" (Mais 1983, 55). But he has been reading the Bible. His main interest is in the story of Samson. He is particularly interested in the complex undercurrents of the relationship between Samson and Delilah, things not mentioned in the Bible. His interest in the story, it seems, is primarily as a study in human relationships; he is drawn to the under-described human drama beneath the surface of the bare biblical account.

It is significant that Jake is interested in this story of a tragic man-woman relationship. Early in the novel we are told that his wife Estella has left him, to run off with a man who, like herself, is from the "lowlands". Jake's story and Samson's are not identical in many respects, but they share a bad experience with a woman. Jake hopes the Bible story will help him to understand his own experience.

But Jake does more than read and reflect on the story. An artist and a blacksmith, he is also making a statue of Samson. For many artists, the creation of art is a way of seeking and finding understanding. The act of creation draws on the artist's deep spiritual resources and personalizes the subject matter profoundly. The making of art as a spiritual practice is a feature of virtually all cultures. But for Jake, the enterprise fails and he destroys the statue, giving it up for worldly use as firewood. He also derives no spiritual understanding from his engagement with the Bible story. His failure to find understanding and meaning in religion is a step in the direction of his suicide which, perhaps significantly, takes place on Sunday, Christianity's holy day.

I turn now to suffering and the meaning of life. Suffering is the lot of virtually all sentient beings. According to legend, the discovery of this appalling fact led Buddha to devote his life to the search for a solution. Buddhism found meaning in the lotus flower which blooms in mud, and concluded that human beings can prosper and flower while drawing sustenance from the mud of suffering. If one cannot make sense of one's inevitable suffering, this can lead to the view that suffering is without use or purpose, and that it renders life meaningless.

Jake seems to lack a positive perspective on his suffering. We are given little insight into his psychology – one of the novel's weaknesses – but the plot tells his story. His misfortunes pile up and as a result he kills himself.

Jake's sufferings are many. He loses his wife Estella to another man, he loses his artistic talent and his health, and he is struck blind by lightning. But he is so alienated from those who love him that their love is powerless to save him. The lightning which blinds him is an act of nature (God). So, apparently, is his loss of health. Other misfortunes are mostly the result of failures of will and character.

Some people in the district regard Jake's blindness as punishment from God because of his pride. Others believe it is God's retaliation for Jake's argument with the parson who visits him after his wife's desertion. Old Mother Coby, the warner woman, declares that God is punishing Jake because, contrary to the First Commandment, he makes graven images.

Jake's suicide makes us aware of the impact this suffering has had on his psyche. We may conclude that he fails to value the remaining good in his life, or to appreciate it more keenly in contrast with his griefs. Unable to see that good can sometimes come out of evil, he fails to be strengthened by his misfortunes. Having failed to make positive use of his suffering, to see the lotus above the mud, so to speak, he heads for the woods with his shotgun.

I will now consider the cultivation of loving relationships as a way of discovering meaning in life. Many people find meaning and purpose in love and friendship. Psychologists and counsellors talk of the importance of having a "support group". Throughout the novel, Jake is surrounded by loving, admiring people, yet he fails to draw strength from them.

Paradoxically, his estranged wife tells Glen and Amos that she left Jake because she loves him. She also tells Amos about a conflict in Jake's character: he dislikes leaning on other people even though he depends on their adulation. This is her explanation for his inability to cultivate loving relationships. We are never given Jake's perspective on his wife's desertion, except his determination not to allow her to return home. We know, mainly through Estella, that he fails to establish a loving and lasting relationship with her. But his suicide speaks much louder than words.

Jake befriends Amos, the accordion-playing hunchback, and thereby helps him to become "somebody". Estella thinks this is one of the best things that Jake has ever done. But in trying to explain Jake to Amos, she also claims that Jake resents the fact that he must depend on Amos for anything. Jake's independence is also a factor in this attempt at friendship. Amos meets the suicidal Jake in the woods and tries to talk him out of doing anything that would make anyone sorry. But he is unable to save his friend's life. When Amos walks away from Jake and tells him goodbye, he is not fully aware of the significance of his words.

Jake's best friend Amos and his loving albeit estranged wife Estella are nearby in the woods when Jake shoots himself. They are holding hands and "waiting for the end of the world" (Mais 1983, 157). Glen and Miriam, the two young lovers who are contrasted with Jake and Estella, are also in the woods. Glen is Jake's assistant in the shop and a generally helpful employee around the house. Miriam is the daughter of Bess, Jake's devoted house-keeper who weeps with the joy of life before Jake leaves for the woods. Miriam also holds the lantern for Jake while he works on his carving. Glen and Miriam are discussing bird shooting and their desire to live, when they hear the gunshot. The sound causes Miriam to shudder, and when Glen asks her why she is shivering, she replies by expressing a folk belief: "Must be something walked over my grave" (p. 159). They are the persons who are closest to Jake, but they are powerless to prevent the tragedy.

Jake is without a sense of the bonds of affection. Neither love nor friendship can save him from suicide. According to Estella, he is incapable of the give-and-take which both require. Therefore neither can help to give meaning to his life.

Many people find meaning in life through the work they do. Through work they make a contribution to society. They may regard their work as merely a job, or they may see it as a vocation or calling.

Jake gets considerable satisfaction from his day-job as a blacksmith. It is a way of helping people. He takes pride in the fact that he can bring a woman relief from her pains simply by fixing her bed. He enjoys the adulation he gets for satisfying the community's needs, and he is satisfied to be carrying on his father's trade. When Massa Butty and Tata Joe visit him, we learn that the community looks up to him as a leader. It thinks he should rise above being a blacksmith to become a foreman for the Public Works or even a school teacher. But Jake is not interested in other work.

In his professional life Jake forges his firmest bonds with his community. The give-and-take which is absent from his personal relationships is present here. The continuation of a family tradition also links him to the past.

This sense of meaning vanishes once he is struck blind by lightning. He loses his profession and his most fulfilling bond with others. Left with no hope of regaining his former job, he chooses suicide as a way out.

But if being a blacksmith is his day-job, sculpture is his vocation. Like most artists trying to find meaning in their creative work, Jake is devoted to his art, but its significance is almost entirely private. There is little, if any, community support. For Mother Coby, as mentioned before, his sculpture is the sinful making of graven images. Massa Butty alludes to the mysterious and useless work Jake is doing in his loft, and is amused by the "dawl baby" Jake carves for Esmeralda. Miriam, who holds a lantern for Jake while he works, cannot see what he sees in the carving.

Jake is an example of the lonely, misunderstood artist who lacks positive engagement with his society. It is perhaps significant that he is a sculptor. Sculpture used to be one of the most important art forms in traditional African societies. Yet there is very little evidence of its survival in Jamaica during the period of slavery. The perishable nature of wood may be part of the explanation, but it is also possible that European prejudice against African religions – which were regarded as witchcraft – also had something to do with it. Jamaican society has taken some time to overcome this deeply ingrained suspicion of sculpture. In fact, one of Jamaica's best known modern wood carvers was accused of witchcraft when he first began to show his work.

For Jake, his carving of Samson is a central part of his life: "The most important thing left to him in life now was his carving and something was happening to that. He could feel it slipping away from him in some intangible manner. It was as though his hand had lost its cunning and faltered when his mind would push ahead" (pp. 69–70). When he carves, Jake feels the same as he does when taking his long solitary walks in the woods: "He got the same feeling from being alone with his carving. Healing went with it, and a sense of stillness and peace. And a feeling that a man is alone in the world and sufficient, and not dependent upon anyone" (p. 75). Mais, who was an artist as well as a writer, writes with understanding about the creative process and its value to the artist.

But Jake's statue is a failure. During a thunderstorm (there are several in the novel), with the moon breaking from behind a cloud, Jake and Amos go up to the loft to view the statue. Jake interprets the statue for Amos, describing Samson as a blind burden-bearer. Amos sees his own deformity as part of that burden. Jake wonders where Samson will set down his burden, and he concludes that the resting place will have to be found in his own brain, even though he cannot find it there. He laments the impotence of his hands. At this point, he perceives a change in the statue and invites Amos to look at it as well. Amos agrees that it is not Samson any more. The statue has undergone a transformation. We are not told what it has become, only what it is not. Shortly after this recognition, Jake is struck blind by the lightning bolt.

The transformed statue is a mystery which the novel does not solve. Mais goes only as far as he needs to make the transformation an indication of Jake's failure to control his material. Sometime later, in a conversation with Amos, Jake contemplates how something created by a man can take on a life of its own. This is an experience, I believe, which is familiar to most creative artists. But, surprisingly, Jake sees it as a loss of talent and artistic power. During a prolonged rainstorm, he takes the carving in a sack to the living room and gives it to Bess and Amos to be used as firewood.

Apparently, Jake does not hold the Nietzschean view that one should live one's life like a work of art (Solomon 1982, 56–57). He does not carry the positive aspects of his art over into his life by living beautifully, or with style, so that his life can be evaluated the way art is.

Blindness and failure to control his material bring Jake's artistic career to an end. One of his main sources of meaning has dried up. It is perhaps significant that he is whittling wood aimlessly – with no artistic purpose – before he fondles the gun he will later use to take his own life.

Finally, I would like to consider Jake's moral life. Traditionally, the moral life is seen as the good life. The question of whether or not the morally good life is more meaningful than the morally bad life dates back at least to Plato. Perhaps, like Plato, the man on the street would argue that it is.

We are told by virtually all of Jake's acquaintances that he is a good man. But apart from his friendship with Amos and his beneficient influence on his community, we are shown little evidence of this. On the contrary, we see that he is proud and unforgiving. In the end, his most significant moral act is suicide.

Can suicide make a life more meaningful? Some philosophers would answer 'yes' to this question. Feldman argues that suicide is morally justified if it makes the world a better place (Feldman 1992). Suicide can be sacrificial and in the interest of others. It can also be heroic – ritual suicide of a certain kind is admired in Japan. It can also be argued that, in some circumstances, suicide may be a rational act: rational in the sense that it is carefully thought out, as well as in the sense that it is done for a reason (Graham 1993, 112). It can also be called rational insofar as it contributes something to the suicide's self-interest.

Jake's suicide is arguably premeditated and thus "rational" in the weakest sense of the word. It is also, arguably, in his self-interest – what Nagel (1987, 92) calls a "negative good" in that it may save him from the anguish of meaninglessness; but given the uncertainty of what happens after death this is not a sure thing. Jake thinks suicide requires courage, so his suicide may be courageous in his own eyes. But it is hardly heroic. I conclude that there is very little evidence in the novel to convince us that Mais wants us to view Jake's suicide as a morally justified and hence meaningful act.

Philosophers and theologians who oppose suicide have argued for centuries that it is against the will of God, contrary to nature and socially harmful. Kant argued that by terminating his or her role as a moral agent the person who commits suicide "roots out" morality (Edwards 2000, 87).

In the novel, it is clear that Jake's suicide will cause a great deal of social harm and suffering. Amos loses an important friend. Estella loses any hope of reunion with her husband. Glen and Bess lose an employer. Miriam loses her means of support. The community loses a respected leader. Clearly Mais wants us to see the suicide as an immoral act that plummets Jake into the depths of meaninglessness.

I do not, however, think Mais wants us to see Jake's descent into meaninglessness as inevitable. It is easy to imagine other possibilities. Perhaps he gives up on religious faith too easily. We know that it is possible to make creative use of our sufferings and that they do not have to lead to despair. None of Jake's misfortunes prevent him from having loving relationships with others. Even though he is blind he can still be a leader in his community. A blind man can still be a sculptor even if it requires changing his material (he obtains modelling clay but does not use it). With the help of Glen, Uriah and George, he can still run his business. Like the blind Milton he could bear his mild yoke and still find meaning in life. That he fails to do any of these things is only an indication of his human imperfection – a fatal mix of hubris and frailty. We sympathize even if we do not condone.

To the blind Jake, the lightning which he sees appears to be black. According to D'Costa (1983, 21) this "suggests a diabolical opposite" of the "divine energy, creativity and justice" which lightning symbolizes. If these notions fit they seem to refer to Jake's loss of artistic creativity and his fall from theological grace. I have encountered the oxymoron of the title elsewhere. Boxers who experience a lot of physical punishment in the ring speak of seeing "dark lights". The notion of dark lights is also to be found in Buddhism. Proulx (1999, 52) writes of a bullrider in a rodeo experiencing "the dark lightning in his gut". I suggest that the black lightning of the book's title is also a symbol used by Mais to represent Jake's state of meaninglessness, irrationality and immorality.

Chapter 3

The Inner Radiance of the Self in
Palace of the Peacock

There is a growing philosophical interest in the novels of Wilson Harris. C.L.R. James (n.d.) sees the influence of Heidegger in them; Benjamin (1989) the influence of Nietzsche. Paget Henry (2000) mentions Gregory Sham's Hegelian reading of this novelist, and goes on to defend his own view that Harris represents what he calls the "poeticist" tradition in Afro-Caribbean philosophy.

I wish to argue that *Palace of the Peacock* engages a philosophical question that is central to virtually all of the world's philosophical traditions, including Western and Eastern philosophy. This is the problem of the self. More specifically, I will try to show that Harris's answer to the question resembles that found in some Eastern philosophies. I will not claim a direct influence, since such claims are difficult to substantiate, but I do believe that Harris gives his own original and distinctly Caribbean slant to the question, and does so in a way that has affinities with Eastern traditions. I am also not claiming that Harris intends the reading I shall give. But, using a reader-response approach (Bressler 1994, 45), I will argue that the novel can bear my interpretation because the fecundity of Harris's imagination leaves his work open to many interpretations.

The problem of the self is the difficulty of answering the following questions: To what does the word *you* refer? A common view is that the word refers to your *self*. But what is the self? Is it your body, your mind, both or neither? The philosophical quest to understand the self is an attempt to grasp the ultimate truth about what we are. It is a fundamental question in metaphysics and epistemology. It is not possible to explore the question in detail here. Suffice it to say that some have regarded the self as an illusion. Others have seen it as the subject of consciousness (Lund 1999), or as a point of view or organizing principle (Blackburn 1999). Some traditions have seen the self as eternal. Others have argued the existence of a non-self.

Along with its intrinsic importance the question is also a fundamental part of other philosophical issues. The question of the selfhood of the fetus is central to the abortion debate. Questions about the rights of the self and the morality of its possible destruction loom large in debates about euthanasia and capital punishment. It is a central part of debates about the question of survival after death. In addition it figures prominently in discussions about issues like self-control, self-cultivation, self-deception, self-realization and self-respect.

I submit that *Palace of the Peacock* ([1960] 1998) can be seen as a symbolic account of a journey into the inner radiance of the self, as a quest myth which employs the motif of a journey. Similar literary works include Homer's *Odyssey*, Dante's *Divine Comedy*, Bunyan's *Pilgrim's Progress* and Conrad's *Heart of Darkness*. Carpentier's *The Lost Steps* is another Caribbean example. Durix (2002) argues that *Palace* is a quest for origins, and mentions its parallels with some of these works.

Palace of the Peacock tells a story of a multi-ethnic crew that travels by boat upriver into the Guyanese heartland. They are commanded by Donne, a violent and domineering colonial conqueror. He is in pursuit of Amerindians, called "the folk", whom he wants to enslave on his coastal plantation. This enterprise, like the search for El Dorado (city of gold) which it echoes, is a quest for material wealth and power. As the crew pursue them, the Amerindians escape into the forest. Some of the crew are killed by the violent river; the others plunge to their death while climbing a steep waterfall. On the eleventh day after leaving the mission the crew members are reunited in the Palace of the Peacock and they have a transcendental experience. Throughout the novel we are given hints that the events described have happened before. Dead characters disappear and reappear in the text. At the end, we are given the impression that it was all a dream.

I turn now to a brief account of the self as it is found in Hinduism and Buddhism. According to Billington (1997), Hindus use the Sanskrit word *atman* to describe the essential self. He finds in Hinduism a dualism of self and body similar to Plato's. For Hindus the *atman* is one with *Brahman,* the ground of being into which it may be absorbed. A persistent feature of Indian philosophy according to Hamilton (2001), is the belief that the quest to understand the self is the most important of aspirations. Self and mind, which are distinct, are among the immaterial substances that make up the universe. There is an old debate in Hinduism between annihilationists who believe that death destroys all traces of the self, and eternalists who believe that the self is a permanent and unchanging substance. Eternalists view the self, as Phillips (1999, 324) puts it, "as the supreme being, infinite, immortal, self-existent, self-aware and intrinsically blissful". It is superior to our ordinary consciousness.

There is some controversy about the Buddhist concept of the self. Apparently there are different interpretations of the Buddha's teachings. According to Billington (1997), Mahayana Buddhism stays close to its Hindu parental conception. Theravada Buddhism remains faithful to what appears to be the Buddha's position. They deny that there is a permanent, unchanging self, believing instead in the non-self and the void.

The position taken by Tibetan Buddhism, which is a branch of Mahayana Buddhism, is relevant to this inquiry. Taking the self to be what some philosophers insist is a mental entity, Rinpoche (1992, 47) describes its discovery as follows: "Just as clouds can be shifted by a strong gust of wind to reveal the shining sun and wide open sky, so, under certain special circumstances, some inspiration may uncover for us glimpses of this nature of mind." He argues that what Hindus call the self, Buddhists call "Buddha nature"; Jews and Christians call it "God"; and Sufi mystics call it "the Hidden Essence".

Let us return to the novel. The metaphor of the river as a symbol of the flow of life and time occurs in many religions and philosophies. In *Palace* it is significant that the characters are travelling upriver, against this flow. In both Hinduism and Buddhism, insight into the nature of the self requires effort, usually yoga, meditation or both. In Indian thought, the personal self becomes attached to the body in order to exhaust both good and bad karma (Ruckmani 2000, 812). Harris's journey to the inner radiance of the self is a difficult upriver struggle which includes climbing a steep and dangerous waterfall.

At first they are driven by the demands of the body: wealth and power. But later on they are guided by an Arawak woman who stands for none of these things. She is close to the pristine primeval spirit of the forest.

Donne and his crew carry the baggage of their various ethnicities: European, African, Indian and their various mixtures. They are burdened by what Webb calls the "alienating effects of the historical process" (quoted in Booker and Jurega 2001, 156). They are a microcosm of Guyana, the Caribbean and of the world.

Near the end of their journey they come upon a waterfall: "They saw in the distance at last a thread of silver lightning that expanded and grew into a veil of smoke. They drew as near as they could and stopped under the cloud. Right and left grew the universal wall of the cliff they knew, and before them the highest waterfall they had ever seen moved and still stood upon the escarpment" (Harris 1998, 100). Their climbing of this cliff symbolizes an elevation of consciousness to the extraordinary level described by the Hindus and Buddhists.

Harris's description of the climbing of the cliff, like the rest of the novel, is surrealist, magic-realist prose-poetry, dense with seemingly hallucinatory images which perhaps only psychoanalytic criticism can decipher. Durix (2002), however, sees biblical allusions in the images of the carpenter and the cross. For our purposes, it is worth pointing out that Donne's reflections on his experiences lead to an insight: "it was the unflinching clarity with which he looked into himself and saw that all his life he had loved no one but himself" (Harris 1998, 107). Donne becomes blind: "he could see nothing and yet he dreamt he saw everything clearer than ever before" (p. 109). The culmination of the climb leads to the perception of an important truth: "the truth was they had all come home at last to the compassion of the nameless unflinching folk" (p. 110). The climb contains images of Donne's own death and resurrection. He and his crew are reborn to a new awareness, to a karmic purification when they finally arrive at the Palace of the Peacock.

That the palace is named after a bird is significant. Campbell (1988, 23), a student of the world's mythologies, tells us that "the bird is symbolic of the release of the spirit from bondage to the earth". Henderson (1964, 147), a Jungian psychologist, tells us that the bird is a symbol of transcendence.

The transcendent, as ordinarily understood, is unknowable and beyond names. But this has never stopped mystics and artists from offering descriptions of encounters with it. Harris ends his novel with some descriptions of the inner radiance of the transcendental self which the crew discovers.

First, it involves a feeling of trust and oneness with the cosmos. The narrator of the novel, also said to be Donne's twin brother and the dreamer of the events described, says: "I had never before looked on the blinding world in this trusting manner – through an eye I shared only with the soul, the soul and mother of the universe" (Harris 1998, 112). There is now a bond of trust between himself and the world. He is in a harmonious relation with reality. The soul (self) partakes in the mother of the universe which resembles what Hindus call *Brahman,* the ground of all being.

Second, this encounter is as blissful as beautiful music. The narrator sees and hears Carroll, a young black man who is a member of the crew, whistling. According to the narrator: "I had never witnessed and heard such sad and such glorious music" (p. 113). Furthermore the music "circumnavigated the globe" (p. 115) suggesting the ancient belief in the music of the spheres. When Carroll's music fills the corridors and ornaments of the palace the narrator says: "I knew it came from a far source within – deeper than every singer knew" (p. 116). The narrator is himself moved to ecstatic singing: "This was the inner music and voice of the peacock I suddenly encountered and echoed and sang as I had never heard myself sing before" (ibid.).

There is a mystical otherworldly quality to the music described by Harris. It creates an experience which is both aesthetic and spiritual and which is shared by all members of the crew in the palace. The music is both sad and glorious, echoing the sad music of humanity which Wordsworth, another philosophical poet, wrote about. The deep source from which it comes, I suggest, is the inner radiance of the self.

Third, there is a feeling of freedom from illusion. According to the narrator: "in the rooms of the palace where we firmly stood – free from the chains of illusion we had made without – the sound that filled us was unlike the link of memory itself. It was the inseparable moment within ourselves of all fulfilment and understanding" (ibid.). In Indian philosophy, the illusory world of human affairs is called *maya;* and one can be liberated from it only through insight into the nature of the self. This seems to be what is happening here. The fulfilment and understanding which the narrator describes also resembles the Buddhist experience of enlightenment.

Fourth, there is a feeling of oneness with fellow human beings. According to the narrator, the selves of all the crew members are united in a single soul: "I felt the faces before me begin to fade and part company from me and from themselves as if our need of another was now fulfilled, and our distance from each other was the distance of a sacrament, the sacrament and embrace we knew in one muse and one undying soul" (p. 117).

This clearly resembles the Hindu belief that ultimately individual selves are absorbed into *Brahman*. Harris's characters discover the spiritual unity underlying all their apparent differences.

Finally, the self is eternal. It has always existed and will always continue to exist. This is summed up in the thought-provoking final sentence of the novel: "Each of us will hold at last in his arms what he had been forever seeking and what he had eternally possessed" (ibid.).

In my interpretation, the novel is about the inner radiance of the Caribbean self. It postulates a spiritual reality underlying all our historical, material, ethnic and political realities. The novel is about the individual but also about our societies. It is about our individual and collective selves. It is one of the Caribbean's most positive and optimistic works.

Booker and Juraga (2001, 156) criticize the ending of the novel as utopian; they claim that it describes a state which is beyond the reach of ordinary Guyanese people.

But as I read it, this is a state aspired to by millions of Hindus and Buddhists, and if Rinpoche is correct, by Christians, Jews and Muslims as well. I think that the elevation of consciousness described in this novel is a universal human goal. (Some even seek it through drugs, leading Marx to describe religion as the opium of the people.) In each of these religions, there is a belief that some human beings have already attained, or will eventually attain, this transcendence.

Chapter 4

Knowledge and Human Understanding in *A House for Mr Biswas*

After reading some literary works, we feel we have a deeper under-standing of the world. Why is this so? Is it because the work discloses some truth about human nature, the human condition, the natural, social, or even transcendental world? Questions about the capacity of art (including fiction) to give us truth, knowledge and understanding are much discussed in aesthetics. Several of the major Western phi-losophers, including Plato, Aristotle and Kant, denied that art can be a source of knowledge, but modern philosophers are more inclined to entertain this possibility (see Zemach 1995; John 2002; Greene 1971; Kieran 2002; Putnam 1993; Novitz 1993).

It is obvious that a novel can give us factual information about the culture it portrays. It can inform us about a society's food, dress, religion, politics and so on. But to give such information is rarely, if ever, the main aim of a novelist. And few of us read novels primarily for this kind of information. Usually we are after a lot more than the cultural details of a society. We praise great art because we think it is something more than sociology or anthropology.

I incline to the view that art can be a source of knowledge and human understanding. It is not my intention to survey all or even most of the claims which have been made in this regard. I shall instead restrict myself to two kinds of knowledge and two kinds of human understanding. These seem to me to be among the most plausible claims. The kinds of knowledge are conceptual knowledge and empathetic knowledge. The two forms of human understanding are Greene's (1971, 202) view that literature can "disclose man in his 'true' pride and potency"; and her view that making sense of experience is a mode of understanding. I shall regard knowledge and understanding as closely related concepts.

I shall argue that we can attain these kinds of knowledge and understanding from the novel *A House for Mr Biswas* by V.S. Naipaul ([1961] 1969). Widely regarded as that author's masterpiece, I think it is one of the most important novels to come out of the West Indies. Naipaul's philosophical importance was recognized by the Swedish Academy when it awarded him the Nobel Prize for literature in 2001; he was described as a "modern *philosophe*". It is a novel of enormous symbolic significance for the peoples of the region.

Let me elaborate on the kinds of knowledge and understanding to be considered. The term "conceptual knowledge" comes from Putnam (1993, 582). It refers to what he calls knowledge of a possibility, and he argues that this is the kind of knowledge we can get from a novel. Zemach (1995, 436) seems to have something similar in mind when he describes a process, said to be familiar to generals, historians and social planners, "whereby we gain insight into the nature of something by imaginatively envisaging how certain actions and initial conditions will influence that thing." He believes that fictional accounts of human nature are the best examples of this process in action. I shall argue that *Biswas* is an imaginative account of a very important West Indian possibility.

The term "empathetic knowledge" comes from Novitz (1993, 585). It is also referred to as "experiential knowledge" (John 2002) and "affective knowledge" (Davies 2002). It refers to knowledge of what it feels like to be in certain situations or to have certain experiences. I shall try to show that in *Biswas*, Naipaul displays extraordinary skill in doing this.

In his *Essay on Man*, Pope writes: "Know then thyself, presume not God to scan; / The proper study of mankind is man" (Allison 1970, 430). In the modern world, the human sciences have taken up this challenge, and investigations into human nature are conducted across many disciplines including philosophy, literature, psychology, biology, politics, sociology and theology. (The relative brevity of the concept of man and the possible disappearance of man is discussed in Foucault [1970].) Earlier I mentioned Greene's view that we expect great literature to "disclose man in his 'true' pride and potency" (1971, 202). I believe that it is mainly through its disclosure of man that literature contributes to human understanding. I shall argue that Greene's words are an exact description of what *Biswas* does. I shall also touch on the question of what the novel says about West Indian man.

Greene also points out that however plausible they may appear, works of imaginative fiction are opaque; they do not refer to a world out there. However, as ways of ordering and making sense of experience they can lead to the kinds of self-reflection that can break down our mental and emotional conventions and give us new ways of seeing. Greene (1971, 212) asks rhetorically: "Is there any capacity more deeply human, more essential for survival in the world?"

In another work, Naipaul (1984, ix–x) describes himself as a "looker" searching for order in the world. I shall argue that *Biswas* is the story of a man trying to make sense of his life by searching for, and finding, order.

The ancient but enduring doctrine of fatalism, and especially Hindu narrations of it, form an important philosophical backdrop to the novel. References to it run through the entire work and I will quote some examples:

> Bipti's father, futile with asthma, propped himself up on his string bed and said, as he always did on unhappy occasions "Fate. There is nothing we can do about it." (Naipaul 1969, 15)

> It was her fate to be childless, but it was also her fate to have married a man who had, at one bound, freed himself from the land and acquired wealth . . . (pp. 31–32)

> More and more too, she bewailed her Fate; when she did this he felt useless and dispirited and, instead of comforting her, went out to look for Alex. (p. 48)

> In many subtle ways, but mainly by her silence, she showed that Mr Biswas, however grotesque, was hers and that she had to make do with what Fate had granted her. (p. 104)

> As your father used to say – she pointed to the photograph on the wall – "What is for you is for you. What is not for you is not for you." (p. 165)

> They have to live with their Fate. (p. 200)

> Her tears were ritual in another way: they were tears for the hardships that had come to her with a husband she had been given by Fate. (p. 202)

> The sisters were puzzled by the erosion, which seemed to them sudden; but they accepted it as part of their new fate. (p. 418)

I have quoted so many references to fate in order to point out that their large number suggests a bearing on authorial intention. Fate is mostly used to explain hardships, but it is also credited with good fortune as well. I have not noticed any fatalistic explanations by Mr Biswas, the protagonist. He seems, in contrast, to be a metaphysical libertarian. The metaphor of paddling his own canoe, which he uses, suggests a man who believes he can influence the future by the use of his free will. It is perhaps significant that the female characters seem more fatalistic than the men.

The novel is a dramatization of the possible. More specifically, it is an account of how a poor descendant of Indian indentured labourers in Trinidad comes to acquire a house of his own. Mr Mohun Biswas, a man so marginalized that the Registrar-General's Department nearly misses his birth, must struggle some forty-six years before he can get to the point where he "found himself in his own house, on his own half-lot of land, his own portion of the earth" (p. 8). The novel is about how a descendant of an uprooted people – as most West Indians are – comes to regard the West Indies as home.

Born in a hut, the wrong way and with six fingers, Mr Biswas is regarded by his parents and the pundit as an unlucky child. Early in his life he has "to leave the only house to which he had some right. For the next thirty-five years he was to be a wanderer with no place he could call his own, with no family except that which he was to attempt to create out of the engulfing world of the Tulsis" (p. 40). Because of his Brahmin caste, he marries into the Tulsi clan, but remains at the fringe of the large family. In his nomadic years, he is to follow many professions: apprentice pundit, sign-writer, shopkeeper, driver or sub-overseer, journalist, unestablished civil servant and failed creative writer.

Early in the novel he tells his mother: "I am going to get a job on my own. And I am going to get my own house too" (p. 67). In his wanderings, he lives in many houses, but he reflects on "how easy it was to think of those houses without him" (p. 131). In none of these houses was he ever more than "a visitor and upsetter of routine".

After his marriage he moves to Hanuman House, home of the Tulsis, including his wife, Shama. It is like a crowded fortress. He is expected to become a part of the clan, but he rebels. They regard him as weak, troublesome and disloyal. But his rebellion is fuelled by his thirst for independence.

The Tulsis set him up as a shopkeeper at The Chase, a settlement of mud huts in the heart of the sugarcane belt. When Shama miraculously produces a meal on their first day there: "He could not look on it as simply food. For the first time a meal had been prepared in a house, which was his own" (p. 146). Although neither the Tulsis nor the villagers, regard the place as his own, he nevertheless puts up a sign naming himself as the proprietor. But neither Mr Biswas nor Shama regard the place as home; they see it as a place of transition. Eventually the shop is destroyed in an "insuranburn" (p. 203) fraud.

His next posting is at the barracks at Green Vale where he is to be a driver or sub-overseer. His resolve to build a house of his own is deepened at the moment of his arrival: "As soon as he saw the barracks Mr Biswas decided that the time had come to build his own house, by whatever means" (p. 266). He fantasizes about the kind of house he wants. He chooses a site on Tulsi land and employs Mr Maclean, an African-Trinidadian carpenter, to build the house. While the house is still under construction, Mr Biswas moves his family into a finished room. A storm of wind and rain destroys the structure; what is left is burnt by the villagers.

After brief stays at Hanuman House and with his relatives in Woodbrook, Mr Biswas's next abode is the Tulsi house in Port of Spain. There his home-making instincts result in his planting a garden. The garden is destroyed by Seth, a dominant authoritarian figure in the Tulsi household.

Although Hanuman House appears as a solid sanctuary at the centre of the novel, we discover that the Tulsis do not regard it, or even Trinidad, as a permanent home, but only as a stage in the journey of their family from India. They leave Hanuman House for Shorthills, a new estate in the mountains of the Northern Range. There, using his savings and the pro-ceeds from his plundering of the Tulsi estate, Mr Biswas decides to have another go at building a house. He finds a suitable site which is unused, isolated and some distance from the road. The unblessed house is com-pleted in less than a month and Mr Biswas and his family move in. During a natural firing of the land, the fire gets out of hand and the house is badly damaged: "Morning revealed the house, still red and raw, in a charred and smoking desolation" (p. 432).

Not long after, the Biswases move back to the Tulsi house in Port of Spain. There, in the crowded house, his children dream of a house of their own. But Mr Biswas loses his vision of the house; he begins to regard houses as things that concern other people. When Owad, Mrs Tulsi's son, is about to return from his studies in England, Mrs Tulsi tells Mr Biswas that he and his family will have to leave to make room for Owad. Owad returns and rubs it in by telling Mr Biswas that in the Soviet Union, as a journalist and writer, he would be given a house. With only six hundred dollars saved, and in a precarious job, Mr Biswas is in a predicament. As a journalist and civil servant, he works at helping the destitute, while being virtually destitute himself.

While in a café, Mr Biswas is approached by a solicitor's clerk who has heard about his problem and who is trying to sell his own home. Mr Biswas visits the house but has many doubts about his ability to buy it. But he decides to take the leap and makes a downpayment. He borrows the rest of the money from Ajodha, a relative, and buys the house.

Having bought the house they discover that it has many flaws. But gradually they forget the inconveniences. They plant a garden and begin feeling at home. He has managed to acquire his own portion of the earth, to live, and die not long after, without becoming one of those who had "been born, unnecessary and unaccommodated" (p. 14).

There are other triumphs for Mr Biswas. His son, Andre, places third in his exams, gets one of the twelve exhibitions, and is awarded a scholarship to study overseas. Sani, his daughter, also gets a scholarship to study abroad; she returns to a good job just as he is about to lose his own. His wife, Shama – one of the most sensitively portrayed characters in the novel, often presented as the voice of reason – gets to the point where she can, without shame, express her loyalty to him and their children instead of to her mother and sisters. Mr Biswas regards this as a triumph nearly as big as the acquisition of his own house.

Empathetic knowledge, the other kind of knowledge we will consider, is more noticeable in *Biswas*, as is perhaps the case in all novels. I shall restrict myself to three examples which seem to me to be especially effective. They all describe what it feels like to be in certain situations.

The first is a description of mental illness. While building his house at Green Vale, Mr Biswas suffers a nervous breakdown. There is a fairly long description of his state of mind leading up to the final crisis. The following is a sample of Naipaul's description of the experience (he himself also suffered a breakdown as a student): "Every morning the period of lucidity lessened. The bed sheet, examined every morning, always testified to a tormented night. Between the beginning of a routine action and the questioning the time of calm grew less. Between the meeting of a familiar person and the questioning there was less and less ease. Until there was no lucidity at all, and all action was irrelevant and futile" (p. 270).

The twisted bedsheet is a powerful image of Biswas's tortured sleep. Naipaul makes us witness the gradual loss of lucidity. Everyday activities such as meetings with familiar persons are questioned; and each time this happens there is a decrease in ease and calm. Most of all, there is the feeling that all actions are irrelevant and futile.

This is an unfortunate state of mind for someone engaged in an activity – housebuilding – which is so important to him. When the unfinished house is severely damaged by wind and rain, an ill Mr Biswas has to be carried to Hanuman House which, for a while, is a veritable sanitarium.

The second is an account of a single moment which is charged with psychological power and meaning. After completing his house at Shorthills, Mr Biswas invites his mother to visit. He had from boyhood been telling her that, after he built his own house, she would come to stay with him. Something she does during her visit makes a deep impression on him and more than any other memory, stays with him long after death. Naipaul describes the moment as follows: "The ground in front of the house had been only partly cleared, and one afternoon, when he had pushed his bicycle up the earth steps on the top of the hill, he saw that part of the ground, which he had left that morning cumbered and unbroken, had been cleared and forked" (pp. 426–27).

Mr Biswas is touched to see his mother helping him to make the house their home. The garden looks to him as one from his long distant past. Poor and unable to give him many of the things of the world, Mr Biswas sees his mother's work in the garden as a gift of herself. The passage is a poignant account of how some actions can be charged with powerful meaning.

The third passage shows what it is like to have one's life changed by an apparently accidental event. I have said that Mr Biswas does not appear to be a fatalist, but he seems aware, as I think most of us are, of how seemingly accidental events can shape our ends. We can get into situations in which we have little choice but to submit to what appears to be the independent flow of life.

After leaving Hanuman House Mr Biswas's main desire is to find a place to spend the night. He is undecided where to go. He thinks of his relatives in the north and the south, but he does not want to go to any of them. A bus pulls up beside him and the conductor seizes his suitcase and shouts the name of Port of Spain as a destination. This is how Mr Biswas responds: "But now, finding himself suddenly separated from his suitcase and hearing the impatience in the conductor's voice, he was cowed and nodded. "Up, up man," the conductor said, and Mr Biswas climbed into the vehicle while the conductor stowed away his suitcase" (p. 308). Except for a short interval, Mr Biswas spends the rest of his life in Port of Spain, where he dies fifteen years later.

Philosophical theories of human nature are all controversial, although their importance as the foundations of political and economic philosophies are well known. Many philosophical issues arising out of the topic have evolved (Stevenson 1974; Shapiro 2000). The issue which seems to have the most bearing on *Biswas* is the question of the extent to which human nature is shaped by social and cultural circumstances.

He is, after all, what Mills (1997b, 54) calls a "historically subordinated" person. Mills coins the word "smadditization", from a Jamaican Creole word, to describe the process by which such persons move from subordination to the recognition of their full personhood. *Biswas* is without the racial affirmation which is part of Mills's meaning of the term. This is perhaps because of the fact that in the Caribbean, East Indians have retained more of their culture and identity than perhaps any other ethnic group.

Mr Biswas is not motivated to become "somebody" in the social-climbing sense. But he does rebel against the domination of the Tulsis, and by extension all the historical and social factors which cause the subordination of people like himself. The novel is about the universal human need for independence and self-respect.

A number of writers have offered views on what makes Mr Biswas a West Indian man. Ormerod thinks it is his nomadic nature (quoted in Boxill 1983, 43). Rohlehr (1977) thinks it is the similarity between Tulsidom and the plantation economies at the heart of West Indian history. Boxill (1983) sees Mr Biswas as a failed artist (creative writer) whose acquisition of a house – a more basic accomplishment – is the start of the West Indian history, the existence of which Naipaul notoriously denies in *The Middle Passage*.

The West Indian significance of the novel, I think, is that it portrays a man who finds an antidote to West Indian rootlessness. It affirms that a West Indian can be at home in the West Indies. It is a portrayal of West Indian man triumphant.

Brathwaite (1977) observes that unlike European novels, the majority of West Indian novels are not about houses; he calls for a kind of "wall-less" West Indian novel as an alternative to the European model. I think that the symbolism of West Indian houses needs to be taken beyond *Biswas*. We notice, for example, that Mr Biswas buys the house, he does not build it. The building, the artistically creative work is done by the solicitor's clerk. Is it significant that he is a restless coloured (mixed race) man? Mr Biswas may be credited with economic creativity, but this is secondary to the creativity of production. Are there any novels about what Naipaul would call history-creation in the West Indies?

More generally, *Biswas* is not only about a triumphant West Indian. It demonstrates what Greene (1971, 202) contends that all great literature should do; it discloses man in his true "pride and potency". Mr Biswas struggles hard to achieve that pride and the novel is a dramatization of his potency.

As a fictional biography – based on the life of Naipaul's father – the novel is largely an attempt at making sense of the life which it portrays. One could focus on the aesthetic and literary order which Naipaul imposes on his material; but that is not my concern here. I shall instead look briefly at Mr Biswas's search for order in his own life.

We may note that he searches for patterns in his life. The following is an example: "A chance encounter had led him to sign-writing. Sign-writing had taken him to Hanuman House and the Tulsis. Sign-writing found him a place in the *Sentinel*" (Naipaul 1969, 323). We engage in this kind of sense-making when we divide our lives into periods, ponder the role of causes and their effects and sometimes see interconnectedness in it all.

And if we believe in free will, that we could have done otherwise, that we could have given our lives a different shape, we may, like Mr Biswas, reflect on what might have been: "What fortune might have been theirs, if only his father had not died, if only he had stuck to the land like his brothers, if he had not gone to Pagotes, not become a sign-writer, not gone to Hanuman House, not married!" (p. 438). Imaginatively contemplating alternatives is part of the process by which we attempt to assess the significance of what did in fact occur.

But it is the purchase of the house that brings Mr Biswas and his family the greatest sense of order: "Soon it seems to the children that they had never lived anywhere but in the tall square house in Sikkim Street. From now on their lives would be ordered, their memories coherent" (p. 581). This passage, too long to be quoted in its entirety, is among the most evocative in the novel. It describes how the memories of the other places where they have lived would become blurred, telescoped or forgotten. It shows how the nerves of memory would be touched by the details of future life, and how the past would be filtered through their experience of this house. To borrow part of the title of another work by Naipaul (1984), in this house the Biswases have found their centre.

Chapter 5

Existentialism and *The Children of Sisyphus*

The title of H. Orlando Patterson's novel *The Children of Sisyphus* (1964) and its epigraph from Albert Camus's *The Myth of Sisyphus* (1955), suggest a link between the Jamaican novel and the well-known work by the existentialist novelist-philosopher. The novel clearly invites an existentialist analysis. I wish to argue, however, that although there are some clear existentialist influences on Patterson's novel, it is perhaps best seen, not as an existentialist novel, but as a pre-existentialist work and as a call for existentialist values.

Given the diversity of its thinkers and literature, a brief definition of existentialism is perhaps impossible. Instead of offering such a definition, I shall summarize three characterizations of it by scholars who have made it their speciality:

1. Lewis Gordon makes what seems like a useful distinction between "philosophy of existence" and "existentialism". The first, he says, is an examination of "freedom, anguish, responsibility, embodied agency, sociality and liberation" (Gordon 1997, 3). These issues, he contends, have concerned humanity for millennia and have been a part of virtually all

cultures, including the cultures of Africa and its diaspora (Gordon 2000, 159–60). The second is a distinctly European historical expression of these concerns which flourished on the Continent in the 1940s and 1950s. He sees them as positive, anti-nihilistic philosophies.

2. After examining the influences of Kierkegaard, Nietzsche, Husserl, Merleau-Ponty and Sartre on the development of existentialism, Warnock (1970) argues that it is a movement with a common ancestry, common interest and present position. In her conclusion she writes: "Many writers on Existentialism see it as, above all, an exploration of human freedom, and a statement of the autonomy of the individual human being" (p. 132). She sees it as a practical philosophy which invites its readers, whether in the form of philosophy or literature, to practise freedom, and to live authentically by taking control of their own lives and facing up to their responsibilities.

3. Priest (2001, 20) in his collection of the writings of Jean-Paul Sartre, the philosopher most associated with existentialism, writes: "there is no set of problems addressed by all and only those thinkers labelled 'existentialist'. However, most of them are interested in some of: What is it to exist? Does existence have a purpose? Is there an objective difference between right and wrong? Are we free? Are we responsible for our own actions? What is the right sort of religious, political or sexual commitment? How should we face death?" All three writers mention freedom and responsibility. I shall take these to be the core existentialist values.

Warnock also regards the methodology of existentialist philosophy as one of its defining characteristics. This is its tendency to approach the abstract via the concrete, the general via the particular. She points out that describing the world in order to discover its meanings is the method typically used by novelists, short-story writers and filmmakers, and that this explains the close link between existentialism and literature. Simone de Beauvoir says somewhere that to be successful, the existentialist philosopher must become a literary artist. A number of them, including Sartre and de Beauvoir, did just that. The impact of existentialism on literature probably exceeds that of any other movement.

Both Camus and Patterson draw on the myth of Sisyphus. It seems as if there are many stories about this mythical character. I will choose the one offered by Hamilton (1940). According to her story, Sisyphus, the King of Corinth, one day saw a magnificent and apparently supernatural eagle carrying a maiden to a nearby island. Sometime later, Asopus, the river god, came to him to ask for help in recovering his daughter Aegina whom, he suspected, had been carried off by Zeus. Sisyphus told him about the eagle and the maiden. This made Zeus very angry and he decided to punish him. He was punished in Hades "by having to try forever to roll a rock uphill which forever rolled back upon him" (p. 298). Sisyphus's truth-telling was also futile. When Asopus went to the island to claim his daughter, he was driven away by Zeus's thunderbolts.

In Camus's meditations on the myth, Sisyphus's fate becomes a metaphor of the human condition. Sisyphus experiences life as absurd; he is the hero of absurdity. This absurdity is something which many people feel keenly. Many experience an absence of God. The inevitability of death causes many to wonder what is the meaning of it all. In Camus's view, we are unable to identify any objective meaning in the universe, and to understand our place in it. He writes: "The absurd is born of this confrontation between the human need and the unreasonable silence of the world" (Camus 1955, 31–32).

But in his book, Camus's primary concern is not to argue to the conclusion that life is absurd. The absurdity of life, rather, is the premise from which he draws certain conclusions. He writes: "Thus I draw from the absurd three consequences which give me revolt, my freedom and my passion" (p. 62). To be condemned to hopeless and futile labour may seem to be the worst possible punishment. But in Camus's view, Sisyphus can surmount his fate by scorning it. Revolt is the most appropriate response to the absurdity of his situation. Camus also believes that in absurdity there is freedom. If man can find no meaning in the universe, this means he is free to create his own. He is therefore better off in an absurd universe. For Camus, joy and happiness are the consequences of recognizing the absurdity of the human condition. According to him: "Happiness and the absurd are true sons of the same earth" (p. 110). In his view, Sisyphus's fate, like ours, is a "lucid invitation to live and to create in the very midst of the desert" (p. 7).

In his reflections on the existentialist philosophies of Africa and the Caribbean, Paget Henry introduces what seems to me to be a useful way of distinguishing between and organizing existential inquiries. He distinguishes between the material world of outer nature, the human world of social life, and the spiritual world of inner nature (Henry 1997, 15). I shall employ this classification, with some modification and criticism, in my analysis of Patterson's novel.

One obvious question posed by Henry's distinctions is the following: Where do we put built environments? They are part of the material world, but since they are the result of man mixing his labour with the natural world, as Locke would put it, they also seem to be part of the social world. At the same time they seem to have much in common with the natural world, at least in metaphysical, ontological terms. Perhaps each of these categories merges into each other. Works of art that are physical objects – paintings, sculptures, architecture – seem to be all three: physical, social and spiritual. I shall, in this inquiry, regard the built environment as part of the social world which borders on the natural, material world.

I begin with the natural world, with what Henry calls "outer nature". There is very little description of natural objects in the novel. But there is a contrast between what Dinah, the protagonist, sees in the Dungle, and what she sees in the suburbs.

The Dungle, which was Kingston's and Jamaica's worst slum in the 1950s, is located beside the sea, which is the dominant natural object in this vicinity. On one occasion it is described as possessing "a raw luscious stinkness" (Patterson 1964, 102). The garbage man sees its movement as being like "the breaking crack of a crocodile's tail" and he sees it as a menace (p. 18). These are all disturbing, negative images.

There is also a description of stars. When they are numerous they are "like eyes of happy ghosts" (p. 102). In Jamaica, ghosts – or duppies as they are also called – are mostly thought of as malevolent beings. If they are happy, it is because of the wretchedness of their victims.

In the Dungle, objects to be seen include: dead pigs and dogs, tangled shrubs and cacti near a cemetery and dodders – also called "love bush" – sucking the life from thorny shrubs.

But in the St Andrew residential area where Dinah works as a household helper for a short while, she sees almond trees, green yards protected by well-manicured hedges. She also sees canaries, ground doves and grass quits which seem safe and secure in their environment.

But it is with the social world, what Gordon calls "sociality", that Patterson is primarily concerned. The social system which he portrays is located in three built environments: the Dungle, the tenement yard and the suburbs. Here is a description of night in the Dungle:

> As the deceptive peace of night fell upon the place, little mysterious kerosene glows began to twinkle from within the shanty hovels, coops and sheds, clustered together like little flocks of wet crows. And the flags of the great Emperor hovering above them, gold and red and green all shading now for oneness, rising every now and then in the wake of the evening breeze, then falling limply, drooped the little flags of glory. (p. 34)

The Dungle, a place of fierce struggle for survival, seems deceptively peaceful. The crows which the hovels, coops and sheds resemble, are Johncrows, Jamaican vultures, which frequent garbage dumps and which share horrifying similarities with the residents of the Dungle. Above this squalor are the flags of hope of the Rastafarian faith.

The tenement yard at Jones Town, to which Dinah moves in her quest for upward mobility, is only a cut above the Dungle: "It turned out that there was very little space between the set of three rooms at the back and the main house. The left side of the main house projected a little from the rest of the building and made up the kitchen and the latrine which Alphanso had told her she should use. A short little paved verandah ran alongside this projection" (p. 62). The buildings are very close to each other showing that the occupants live very close together and have very little privacy. Many people share the same kitchen and latrine.

In contrast, here is a description of Mrs Watkins's St Andrew house where Dinah works as a helper: "The house was a large 'L'-shaped green and white structure with a flat roof. It was situated a little way in from the road on one of the little gradients at the foot of the hill. Most of the front of the yard was taken up with a pear-shaped swimming pool" (p. 120). The house is in the foothills; Kingston is set against a backdrop of mountains. We are told its shape, colours and design. The presence of a swimming pool tells us that it is in an upper-middle-class neighbourhood.

The human world that occupies these built environments is the main focus of the novel. It portrays the rituals and beliefs of the Rastafarians who live in the Dungle. Rastafarianism is a religion of Jamaican origin. The novel also describes the beliefs and practices of Revivalism, a Jamaican Afro-Christian religious sect which, like the tenement yard, operates a cut above the Dungle. It also describes the harsh realities of prostitution, Jamaica's widespread unemployment, and the impotence and hypocrisy of political leaders. It portrays life in overcrowded and sometimes violent tenement yards, and contrasts this with brief glimpses of middle-class life in Jamaica.

In this social world, Patterson sees a Sisyphean cycle. Dinah, a prostitute who lives in the Dungle, is determined to leave and to improve her condition in the world. Mabel, another resident of the Dungle, also tries to leave. But they are forced to return by a seemingly fated inevitability. Brother Solomon, the defrocked Church of England priest turned spiritual leader of the Rastafarians in the Dungle, says: "Is only me who can see the dreary circle going round and round" (p. 193). According to Rachael, the old woman: "Is not wha' yu wan' fe do, me gal, is wha' yu 'ave fe do" (p. 31). She is fatalistic; she believes that God has placed them in the Dungle for a reason. The Sisyphean cycle is also linked to Jamaican folklore. Mabel speaks of getting an obeah man to set the Dungle on Dinah so she will be unable to leave. Mrs Davis, another resident in the tenement yard, tells Dinah about "oil-o'fall-back" which has the power to put a spirit on a person so that "no matter how near you reach your goal you mus' tumble back down" (p. 115). Dinah sees a "frightening compulsion" about life in the Dungle (p. 96).

The plot of the novel demonstrates the Sisyphean cycle. Dinah tries to leave the Dungle by going to live with Alphanso, a policeman, in a tenement yard in Jones Town. She also manages to secure a job as a household helper in the suburbs. The move brings its own problems and does not satisfy her. At Mrs Davis's suggestion, she turns to Shepherd John, the revivalist preacher, who invites her to live at his church. But his interest in her is more sexual than spiritual. She and the Shepherd are about to migrate to England, the final fulfilment of her aspirations, when tragedy strikes. The jealous Elder Mother stabs Shepherd John and places the blame on Dinah who is attacked by the church members. Badly injured and bleeding, Dinah flees back to the Dungle and to her death.

A novel that portrays the rituals and beliefs of these religions should have something to say about what Henry calls "the spiritual world of inner nature". But it is in this domain that the author's vision is perhaps at its bleakest. The quest for spiritual illumination seems even more futile than the quest for social mobility. I shall deal first with Dinah's Revivalism and then with Brother Solomon's Rastafarianism.

Patterson provides very thorough descriptions of the sights, sounds and smells of a Revivalist church. He describes many of their beliefs and rituals. Aided by his assistants, Shepherd John takes Dinah through what are said to be purification rites. She is initiated into "all the wisdom and mysteries of the Church" (p. 154). She has a partial religious experience which leads to flagellation by Shepherd John and culminates in their sexual union. "His flesh stole into her like a spirit" (p. 164). But it is only "like" a spirit, because as far as Dinah is concerned there is no experience of the sacred or any transcendence of her humanity.

During one of their services Dinah observes that their singing, dancing and shedding of the misery of their lives leads only to "the dead nothingness of joy" (p. 145). During her purification rite, she reasons that if sin is God's enemy, then the sins of whoring, poverty, filth and hate should be as powerful as God. Yet she feels no such power. The barren patch outside on which she is meditating during one of the rites recedes into a "vast eternal nothingness" and only the moment in time seems real (p. 151). This concept of nothingness is part of the spiritual failures of both Revivalism and Rastafarianism. I will say more about it later.

Brother Solomon is portrayed as a Rastafarian philosopher for whom, as he says, philosophizing is worrying about one's neck or worrying about whether or not one's neck is worth worrying about. The neck imagery which he uses precedes his own suicide by hanging.

In the opening sentence of *The Myth of Sisyphus*, Camus famously declares suicide the only serious philosophical problem. In Patterson's novel, Solomon's suicide is one of the climactic events. In his meditations on suicide he calls it "the supreme reason" (p. 193). Before committing the act he says: "The sky is so empty tonight, Brother. So empty. Never saw it so empty. It never turn me round so much with nothing as tonight" (pp. 191–92). It is worth noting that he refers to nothingness elsewhere. Once, while smoking his chillum pipe – Rastafarians regard ganja as a holy weed which gives wisdom – he experiences consciousness melting "away into nothingness" (p. 56). And shortly before committing suicide "his wide, black eyes fixed upon the frame of dark-blue nothingness" (p. 195).

The empty sky which Solomon sees may be seen as a portrayal of the absence of objective meaning in the universe which is at the heart of Camus's view of absurdity. But Solomon and Camus draw different conclusions from this absurdity. Solomon sees it as a reason for suicide. But Camus rejects the legitimacy of suicide (Camus 1955, 7).

Both Solomon and Camus focus on a particular moment in the Sisyphean cycle. While the Rastafarians await the arrival of ships to take them back to Africa (Solomon has lied to them about the ships), Solomon claims that "For the moment they are conquerors. For the moment they have cheated the dreary circle" (Patterson 1964, 194). While they enjoy this illusory happiness they are, he says, like gods.

Camus focuses on the pause, the moment before Sisyphus begins his descent to the bottom of the hill. According to Camus: "At each of those moments when he leaves the heights and gradually sinks towards the lairs of the gods, he is superior to his fate. He is stronger than his rock" (Camus 1955, 109). At this moment, for Camus, "His fate belongs to him. His rock is his thing" (p. 116). He can scorn his fate and thereby triumph over it.

The moment which Solomon ascribes to the Rastafarian is one of delusion and defeat. The moment which Camus ascribes to Sisyphus is one of deep insight and triumph.

Sometimes Solomon talks as if he has read some existentialist literature. Consider the following quotation: "Hear me, Brother, to seek after God, to seek for some meaning, some essence, is unreality twice times over" (Patterson 1964, 194). This is a gesture towards atheistic existentialism in its denial of the value of the search for God, meaning and essence. Again, Solomon does not follow Camus into believing in the joyous creation of meaning, even if this meaning perishes at death.

I come now to the concept of nothingness which is part of the spiritual experience of both Dinah and Solomon. Nothingness is an important concept for some existentialists, especially Sartre. One of his major works is titled *Being and Nothingness* (1966). He identifies nothingness with consciousness. But although he spells out why he thinks consciousness is nothingness – for example, its insubstantiality, its translucency, its freedom (Oaklander 1992, 281) – there is very little indication of the content of Dinah's and Solomon's experience of it. They are certainly not instances of Sartrean freedom.

Neither do they seem to be instances of the concept of emptiness in Buddhist philosophy. According to this doctrine, one may be empty of defilement, subject-object dualism, causality, a self, and so on (Williams 2000, 108). But given the Afro-Christian identity of both Revivalism and Rastafarianism, it is doubtful if such a view is intended. Buddhists, of course, regard their teachings as fundamental to all religions. What this concept of nothingness is intended to convey, it seems, is that both Dinah and Solomon are spiritual failures.

In the definition of philosophy of existence given earlier, Gordon identifies anguish as one of its main themes. There is plenty of both physical and mental pain portrayed in the novel. From Solomon, who believes that his tortured soul is part of what it means to be human, to Dinah's futile struggle and fatal injuries; from the frustration of the jobless mob to the imminent and massive disappointment of the Rastafarians; from Mabel's failure to Mary's madness – there is much that fits the dictionary definition of the word "anguish".

But for existentialist philosophers – especially Sartre – the term has another meaning. For them, to experience anguish is to be conscious of one's freedom. But the agony of choice is not a central issue in this novel.

Many writers on existentialism, as we have seen, regard freedom and responsibility as the central themes of existentialist philosophy. Few, if any, of the characters in this novel see themselves as free agents who are responsible for their condition. For Rachael, it is the will of God. For the Rastafarians, it is the sins of their forefathers. Dinah, as mentioned before, sees it as "frightening compulsion" in the poverty of the Dungle. The author seems to espouse a kind of social determinism. To many existentialist philosophers, especially Sartre, persons holding such a view are guilty of "bad faith", the term used for a failure to recognize one's freedom and to accept responsibility for one's life. This novel is not about freedom and liberation; it is about unfreedom. There is nothing like Sartre's radical libertarianism: "man is condemned to be free" (Priest 2001, 32). Crosby (2000), in opposition to Gordon's view, posits that there is such a philosophy as existential nihilism. This philosophy "negates the meaning of human life, judging it to be irremediably pointless, futile and absurd" (pp. 32–33).

The above may seem like a perfect description of *The Children of Sisyphus*. Yet in spite of its bleak outlook and what Booker and Juraga (2001) call its philosophy of despair, I will argue that this is not a nihilistic novel. According to Nussbaum, "Built into the very structure of a novel is a certain conception of what matters" (Nussbaum 1990, 26). It might be stretching it to say that Nussbaum's view applies to all novels, as this would rule out the possibility of a nihilistic novel, and it may be the case that there are such novels. My claim here is only that Nussbaum's view applies to Patterson's novel. I think it would be incorrect to say that nothing matters to the author. If, as Socrates tells us, ethics is the study of how we ought to live, it is also, by implication, the study of how we ought not to live. And this, it seems to me, is what this novel sets out to tell us. Consider, for example, its opening sentence: " 'Oh, what a life, what a worthless, lousy, dirty life,' one of them cursed beneath his breath, staring at the tick that was sucking the life from the hoary grey ear of the donkey that pulled the cart" (Patterson 1964, 9). The novel is not a negation of moral value. It is an expression of moral outrage at the conditions existing in parts of Kingston at the time in which it is set.

In 1957, Camus was awarded the Nobel Prize for literature. He was commended for illuminating "the problems of the human conscience in our times" (Sprintzer 2000, 121). Patterson, I suggest, follows Camus in trying to awaken the Jamaican social conscience. But while he follows Camus sociologically, he does not follow him philosophically. In Patterson's novel there is none of the existential revolt, freedom and passion that Camus deduces from the absurd.

I submit that Patterson portrays the "frightening compulsion" of social determinism not to endorse the form it takes in the novel, but to draw attention to its possible destructiveness. The Dungle is condemned because it frustrates existentialist values like freedom and self-determination. The portrayal of such values at work in Jamaican society would result in a novel of a very different kind – a genuine existentialist novel. It is interesting to note that Patterson went on to make the study of the concept of freedom a central part of his scholarly investigations. (See his *Freedom*, volume 1: *Freedom in the Making of Western Culture*.) It is in this sense that I say that in terms of Patterson's intellectual biography, his novel *The Children of Sisyphus* is "pre-existentialist" and a call for existentialist values in Jamaican society.

Chapter 6

Tragic Vision in *Wide Sargasso Sea*

While V.S. Naipaul's *A House for Mr Biswas* is the story of a man who succeeds in making the West Indies his home, Jean Rhys's *Wide Sargasso Sea* ([1966] 1997) is an account of a woman who is unable to do so. Like the Sargasso Sea, a mass of seaweed surrounded by swirling currents in the Atlantic Ocean, the novel's troubled heroine is suspended between England and the West Indies and belongs fully to neither.

This novel is a good example of what literary theorists call "intertextuality": the view that literary works "are made out of other works" (Culler 1997, 33). Jean Rhys read Charlotte Brontë's *Jane Eyre* and was not satisfied with its treatment of Bertha Antoinetta Mason, Rochester's mad wife whom he keeps secretly confined in an attic at Thornfield Hall. Rhys resolved to write a more satisfactory account of this character, to tell her story from the point of view of someone more familiar with the history, culture and landscape that shaped her. *Wide Sargasso Sea* can stand on its own, but viewing it as a "reinscription" of aspects of Brontë's book as Spivak (1995) does, or as a dialogic "counterdiscourse" to it, as Griffith (1998) does, adds another dimension to the interest which literary critics have taken in it.

It is well known that images of the Caribbean appeared in English literature for several centuries before the appearance of an indigenous West Indian literature. One of the most widely discussed instances of this, at least in the Caribbean, is the virtually archetypal significance which Prospero and Caliban (in Shakespeare's *The Tempest*) have assumed in literary discourse and other forms of thought in the Caribbean. The West Indian response to such portrayals is part of what has come to be called the postcolonial ethos, both in creative writing as well as in literary criticism. Works like *Wide Sargasso Sea*, and the critical studies based on them, seek to challenge, revise and transform the earlier colonial images.

My main concern here is to examine this novel as a focus of moral reflection. In spite of its long history, it seems as if ethical approaches to literature have been out of favour in the West for a large part of the second half of the twentieth century (Parker 1998). The fear of ideological bias, and the philosophical morass of ethical relativism, seem to be two of the reasons why so many literary critics have tried to stay clear of the ethical questions raised and explored in literature. A similar dodging of the normative, and an emphasis on the meta-ethical, marks early-twentieth-century analytical moral philosophy. Many watched sadly as two of the big values – goodness and beauty – appeared to be retreating from the academy. But it seems to me that the Socratic view of ethics – as the study of how we ought to live – is so important that those literary critics and philosophers who ignore it are guilty of a dereliction of duty. Philosophy has long since returned to the investigation of normative issues, and areas like applied ethics are now flourishing. Happily, as Parker (1998) puts it, there is also a "turn to ethics" in literary criticism. Some influences on this turn include Martha Nussbaum (1990) and Iris Murdoch (Diamond 1998, 85). Nussbaum argues that moral philosophy needs novels since only they can adequately express certain moral experiences. She argues, too, that even the form of a novel can convey something of the novelist's conception of how we should live. Murdoch contends that literature can portray the density of human life in ways that philosophy cannot, and is at the same time more accessible than academic philosophy. McGinn argues that the ethical is embedded in the fictional, and contrasts the rule-governed "scientific" approach to moral education with Jesus' literary approach through the use of parables. In his view, "literature is where moral thinking lives and breathes" (McGinn 1997, vi). I agree that ethical enquiry benefits when philosophy's emphasis on logic, argument and generality is combined with literature's power to portray the depth, resonance and richness of lived moral experience.

In spite of its small size, *Wide Sargasso Sea* deals with an impressive range of issues including history, gender, race, madness, alienation, oppression, religion and violence. My main concern here is to examine it as a West Indian tragedy. I shall do so by first focusing on a number of ethical questions which it raises, including the subjection of women (the phrase is from J.S. Mill); the treatment of the mentally ill or of persons regarded as such; and alienation as a psychological evil. I shall then bring these to bear on the novel's tragic vision. After this I will examine the novel's position as to whether some forms of violence are morally permissible. I shall conclude with some observations on the moral significance of the novel's form.

The struggle by feminists (female and male) against the almost universal and historically pervasive subjection of women by men is certainly a central moral issue of both past and present times. The novel, which is perhaps the literary genre in which women have excelled most, and the one for which they probably make the largest readership, has become part of this struggle. This is becoming increasingly true of the Caribbean, where, although often ignored and under-studied, according to Mordecai and Wilson (1989), women's writing is nevertheless flourishing. Some critics have questioned whether or not *Wide Sargasso Sea* is a West Indian novel. My own view is that there is evidence of a West Indian sensibility on virtually every page. Jean Rhys was born in Dominica and left there as an adolescent. The impact of the region on her psyche is evident in the book. I have no hesitation in regarding it as a West Indian novel. There is also the question of its significance. For Ramchand (2004), it is an expression of the "terrified consciousness" of white Creole writers. To others, its subject matter is marginal to the folk culture which they see as the heartland of West Indian social reality. Others, like O'Callaghan (1996), have argued that white Creole women writers like Rhys have a perception of Caribbean historical realities which is not available to other West Indian writers. I agree with O'Callaghan, and believe this is also true of all other ethnic minorities in the region.

This novel is a powerful portrayal of the possible tragic consequences of patriarchy, which I take to be the sum of all material, sexual and ideological efforts to dominate women. In the novel, one example of this is the way that existing English law allows an unnamed man, whom we recognize as Rochester from *Jane Eyre*, to be paid a dowry of thirty thousand pounds to marry Antoinette and, as a result, to own all her assets. This domination plays a critical role in her eventual alienation, "madness", and the dehumanizing control of her body which we see in her transportation and incarceration. Antoinette, however, rebels against her subjection to this law. When her stepfather Mason visits her in the attic to which she has been confined, he says: "I cannot interfere legally between yourself and your husband" (Rhys 1997, 119–20). Antoinette flies at him with a knife, and when he tries to twist it out of her hand, she bites him. Her rebellion is clearly directed against what she regards as an immoral law.

Shortly after their honeymoon in one of the Windward Islands, Antoinette is sexually rejected by Rochester. He turns to Amelie, a servant girl who is portrayed as a sexy mulatto. But he has no respect for her either, seeing her as "sly, spiteful and malignant" (p. 39). He clearly sees women as objects to be exploited for money and sex. The psychological damage of Rochester's rejection is another factor in the process of Antoinette's decline.

Rochester's determination to subjugate Antoinette is also evident in his persistence in calling her "Bertha" (her name from *Jane Eyre*). Few things are more closely linked to a person's sense of self than his or her name. Rochester's patriarchal onomastics – Antoinette calls it English obeah – is a strategy aimed at controlling her innermost being.

We also see patriarchy in her mother's dependence on men. After the death of her allegedly philandering husband, Annette has to marry Mason to avoid economic ruin. But this does not save her. The historical and social doings of men – slavery, black revolt – will take her to madness, sexual abuse and death.

Christophine, who is Antoinette's former nurse in Jamaica, and her servant and confidante on the honeymoon island, once suffered the indignity of being given to Annette, Antoinette's mother, as a wedding present. Portrayed as a strong character, and perhaps as a contrast to Antoinette, she is a defiant woman of knowledge who stands up to Rochester. But, like the alleged witches in Europe, she is both feared and persecuted, and was once reportedly jailed for practising obeah. Rochester goes to great lengths to try to subjugate and destroy her.

It is perhaps part of Rhys's critique of patriarchy that although Rochester succeeds in achieving wealth and power, he does not, in this novel, achieve any effective or spiritual consolations. The subjection of women, one might say, can also be a disadvantage to men.

The question of how to treat persons deemed to be "mad" is and has been an important moral issue for nearly every society. Some ancient societies saw the insane as possessed or wicked (Neander 2000). Gutting (1994, 48), in his reading of Foucault's study of the evolution of attitudes to madness in Europe, concludes that Foucault sees madness "as a variable social construct, not as a historical scientific given, and sees the history of madness as an essential part of the history of reason". Foucault's study, according to Lechte (1994), ranges over views of the mad person as the paradigm of the socially excluded person, as a wanderer, as a source of truth, wisdom and social criticism, as the embodiment of silence and unreason, as any kind of social outcast, to the medicalization of madness in the nineteenth century. Foucault argues that the view of madness as mental illness, rather than as a police matter, came not because of great discoveries in medicine, but because of increasing concern with individual rights, and a shift in seeing the asylum as therapeutic rather than as punitive.

But the view that there is such a thing as mental illness has been challenged by Szasz (1975). He argues that if mental illnesses are brain diseases, then the term is a Rylean "category mistake", since the brain is part of the body. If they are psychological (non-biological) personality disorders then the term is metaphorical, like "sick economy" or "sick joke". If it is a term which psychiatrists are licensed by the state to apply, then it is giving some persons the authority to engage in name-calling, suspect classifications, and to incarcerate other persons against their will. These arguments suggest that the term is not as easily defined as it seems, and is in need of serious philosophical analysis. Here I am concerned only with some of its ethical aspects.

Wide Sargasso Sea is set in the first half of the nineteenth century, apparently before the medicalization of madness. The treatment meted out to Antoinette is sexual and romantic rejection followed by forced transportation to England and incarceration there. Her hostile treatment begins early in Jamaica, the land of her birth. There she is stigmatized by the albino (himself suffering from a biological impediment) and the black girl (herself a victim of discrimination and exploitation); they tell her she is being sent to the convent in Spanish Town because her Aunt Cora does not want a potentially mad person in her house. Daniel Cosway, the mulatto on the honeymoon island who also claims to be her half-brother, thinks that madness in her family is a condition that is terrible enough to be used for blackmail; he wants Rochester to pay him five hundred pounds to keep it a secret.

Is Antoinette mentally ill? The answer to this question is perhaps best left to persons licensed by the state to make this kind of judgement.

Psychoanalytical critics may also have much to say about the subject. The rest of us, however, are also entitled to our opinions.

During her confinement, Antoinette says she hears a sound in her head. Hearing voices, a claim made by many prophets and saints, is said to be a symptom of schizophrenia. Perhaps Rhys intends it to be read as such. Antoinette's mother is also portrayed as having a mental breakdown, and since some mental illnesses are said to have a genetic component, this too may be seen as evidence for the protagonist's madness. Presumably, mother and daughter may be seen as parallel cases of an inherited constitutional disposition which breaks under great stress. Annette's breakdown is precipitated by the social and economic decline caused by the abolition of slavery, the death of her first husband, and the collapse of her second marriage after Coulibri is burned by former slaves – developments which result in her being cast out of her former home. Antoinette's breakdown, then, may be the result of these events added to the failure of her marriage, and the sequence of dislocations she has suffered, both from Jamaica and from the honeymoon island which she previously loved.

But there is another side to the coin. Foucault seems to suggest that the history of madness is the history of unreason, to be contrasted with the history of reason or rationality. But "unreason" does not seem the right term to apply to Antoinette's thoughts and actions. In her final narrative, she says she knows that she is in the attic at Thornfield Hall for a reason, and she concludes that this reason is to set fire to the building. We are not given access to the process of her reasoning, but as readers of the novel we already know what these reasons are. I shall say more about the meaning of her intended arson later, but here we find her a thinking and reflective character who is concerned about her own selfhood and integrity. In *Jane Eyre*, she is portrayed as the source of spooky Gothic horror. But Rhys's novel does not support that view of her: "I did not want to see that ghost of a woman who they say haunts this place" (Rhys 1997, 122). There is very little evidence of derangement in her reflections on her past and present experiences.

The question of the moral responsibility of mentally ill persons is another much debated philosophical issue. In many jurisdictions, anyone deemed to be criminally insane is not held accountable for their actions. Szasz opposes this practice. If Antoinette is not morally responsible for burning down Thornfield Hall, this has important implications for the meaning of the novel.

I think Rhys wants her to be regarded as morally responsible, even though she seems to be ambivalent about whether or not Antoinette is mentally ill. Either conclusion makes an important statement. If Antoinette is not mentally ill, then she is an "innocent" victim of social prejudices. If she is mentally ill, then she is a victim of society's harsh treatment. Either way, her treatment explains her disbelief in justice: " 'Justice,' she said. 'I've heard that word. It is a cold word. I tried it out,' she said, still speaking in a low voice. 'I wrote it down several times and always it looked like a damn cold lie to me. There is no justice'" (p. 94).

Artistic portrayals of the mentally ill are often unscientific and sensationalist. Hollywood films often portray them as violent, while critics of those films point out that these persons are more likely to be the victims of violence than the perpetrators of it. The film *A Beautiful Mind* suggests that new approaches to portraying this subject matter may be developing.

Rhys, writing in the twentieth century, portrays her character as a human being, a victim, perhaps of heredity as well as of historical and social circumstances. Significantly, Antoinette is portrayed as someone with a spirit of self-affirmation which Grace Poole, her guard, admires. Rhys's approach is consistent with Szasz's demand for greater respect for the rights and freedoms of persons deemed insane. The increasing emphasis on family and community-based treatment, rather than on incarceration, seems to be moving in this direction. A balance has to be found, I think, between a society's right to self-preservation, which some philosophers see as the source of morality, and the need to respect the human rights of all its members.

In addition to her subjugation on grounds of gender, and her stigmatization and incarceration on grounds of madness, Antoinette also suffers severe alienation. I use the word not in its Marxist sense, but to refer to the experience of separation, estrangement and rootlessness. Antoinette is alienated both from the Caribbean and English landscapes, and from virtually all the people in her life.

As a child she feels safe in the Caribbean. She describes Coulibri as "the most beautiful place in the world" (p. 83). The tree of life which she sees in their garden is a promise of prosperity. But she also notices that the garden is growing wild. The snake-like orchid and the strong, sweet smell of the flowers create a feeling of foreboding. She avoids the orchid, but her bond with the Caribbean landscape continues on the honeymoon island: "The sky was dark blue through the dark green mango leaves, and I thought, 'This is my place and this is where I belong and this is where I wish to stay'" (p. 68).

The break begins with Rochester's sexual and emotional rejection of her. She says of the island: "But I loved the place and you have made it into a place I hate. I used to think that if everything else went out of my life I would still have this, and now you have spoilt it" (p. 95). She has come to hate the place as much as she hates Rochester, and she declares that before she dies she will show him the extent of her hatred.

Her images of the English landscape come mainly from geography books. She imagines "cool green leaves in the short cool summer. Summer. There are fields of corn like sugar-cane fields, but gold-colour and not so tall. After summer the trees are bare, then winter and snow" (Rhys 1997, 70). But she already has a premonition of a sense of unbelonging, of being excluded there in a cold room with red curtains. When she does get to England she believes they have lost their way and ended somewhere else. In her experience of what she believes is England: "There was grass and olive-green water and tall trees looking into the water. This, I thought, is England. If I could be here I could be well again and the sound in my head would stop" (p. 119). She thinks of England as a potentially healing place. But for her it is not.

Before she sets out to set fire to Thornfield Hall, memories of the Caribbean landscape come back to her. Her red dress reminds her of fire, sunset and the flowers of the flamboyant tree which, when it is in bloom is believed in the Caribbean to lift the souls of persons buried underneath it. The dress has the smell of vetivert, frangipani, cinnamon, lime trees, sun and rain. In the dream which precedes the climax of the novel she sees "orchids and stephanotis and the jasmine and the tree of life in flames"; she also sees "bamboos and the tree ferns, the gold ferns and the silver, and the soft green velvet of the moss on the garden wall" (p. 123). As a result of her separation, the Caribbean landscape exists for her now only in memory; but these memories seem especially vivid just before her death.

Antoinette is also unable to make any meaningful connection with her husband Rochester. Before marrying him she has a dream of precognition in which she is walking through a forest with a man who hates her. In the dream, her beautiful white dress trails on the ground. After the wedding, she begins to see Rochester as a scornful and silent man.

In his narrative, Rochester admits that in courting her he was only playing a role. He finds her pretty but sees her dark eyes as sad and alien. He is horrified at the thought that she might be partly black. After he rejects her he says: "I drew the sheet over her gently as if I covered a dead girl" (p. 88).

Rochester is also unable to connect with the Caribbean landscape which he sees as dream-like, indifferent or excessive, wild, menacing and cruel. He sees sadness in a leaning coconut tree, and hears it in the song of a bird. He says: "I hated its beauty and its magic and the secret I would never know" (p. 111).

A central part of the experience of Europeans in the Caribbean is their encounter with Africans, and the offspring of any unions that arise from this encounter. *Wide Sargasso Sea* is set in the period shortly after the abolition of slavery, and the novel explores some of the difficulties of this relationship. Antoinette has both positive and negative experiences with these other persons, but here, too, she is unable to maintain a meaningful and enduring connection with any of them.

The abolition of slavery and the death of her father result in the decline of Coulibri Estate. Now they eat salt fish, wear shabby clothes and catch water with calabashes in their leaky old home. The recently freed blacks believe that only rich whites are real white people, so they dub the Cosways "white niggers". A little black girl follows Antoinette and calls after her: "White cockroach go away, go away. Nobody want you, go away" (p. 9).

The gulf between Antoinette and her black countrymen is nowhere more evident than in her relationship with Tia, her black playmate. After a disagreement over a bet, Antoinette calls her a "cheating nigger" (Rhys 1997, 10). She has already internalized some of the racism of her elders. Then, after they bathe together in the pool, and Tia takes away her dress, Antoinette puts on Tia's dress and goes home in it. Her mother orders the nurse Christophine to burn the dress. When the blacks start burning down Coulibri – their reason will be discussed later – they all look the same to Antoinette. But she picks out Tia in the crowd, the girl with whom she had shared food, bed and play. She wants to live with her and be like her. She does not want to leave Coulibri. She wants to cling to Tia for she is all that is left of her past life there. But this hope is not realized:

> When I was close I saw the jagged stone in her hand but I did not see her throw it. I did not feel it either, only something wet, running down my face. I looked at her and I saw her face crumple up as she began to cry. We stared at each other, blood on my face, tears on hers. It was as if I saw myself. Like in a looking glass. (p. 24)

In some respects they are like mirror images of each other, but they are separated by a hurled stone of anger and resentment, and blood and tears.

Tia reappears to Antoinette in the dream she has before the climax of the novel. "But when I looked over the edge I saw the pool at Coulibri. Tia was there. She beckoned to me and when I hesitated she laughed. I heard her say, 'You frightened?'" (p. 124). She shouts Tia's name before she jumps over the edge and wakes up. Tia beckons to her to make the leap that would reunite them, and laughs when she sees that the prospect frightens Antoinette. (Does this signify a terrified consciousness?) Antoinette does jump, if only in a dream, and it is significant, surely, that she shouts Tia's name before she does so.

Antoinette's warmest relationship is with Christophine, her Martinican-born nurse, who is described as "blue-black with a thin face and straight features" and who wore a black dress, heavy gold earrings and a yellow handkerchief – carefully tied with the two high points in front" (p. 7). Christophine is a source of strength for Antoinette who seeks her advice, and asks her for a love-potion to regain Rochester's interest. The love powder appears to energize Rochester's sexual feelings, but it has a negative effect on his health and emotions. However, as a teenager, after seeing a black man intoxicate and then kiss her ill mother, Antoinette angrily calls Christophine "a damned black devil from Hell" (p. 86). She also comes to question the wisdom of taking advice from Christophine: "I stared at her, thinking, 'But how can she know the best thing for me to do, this ignorant, obstinate old Negro woman, who is not certain if there is such a place as England?'" (p. 70). After losing confidence in Christophine's wisdom, Antoinette refuses to take her advice to leave Rochester.

Antoinette has coloured (mixed race) relatives, but forms no mature or mutually sustaining relationship with any of them. Mr Mason's lectures make her feel "shy" about them (p. 28). Daniel Cosway's true identity is a mystery and there are different opinions as to who he really is. He is portrayed as an objectionable character who may be a fraud. There is also an undeveloped suggestion of a romantic link between Antoinette and Sandi.

In sum, Antoinette has sustaining relations with no place and with no one. She is without a strong sense of personal identity: "So between you I often wonder who I am and where is my country and where I belong and why was I ever born at all" (p. 64). Antoinette sums up her alienation when she tells Rochester: "I wish to stay here in the dark . . . where I belong" (p. 87).

Antoinette's tragedy is her subjection, stigmatization and incarceration for madness, and her severe alienation. But when it is examined against the background of tragedy as a literary genre, a few more things may be said about this novel. Most people associate the term "tragedy" with drama, especially some of the most highly regarded plays of ancient Greece and Elizabethan England. But the term has also been applied to novels like Melville's *Moby Dick*. Philosophical interest in tragedy is at least as old as the fourth century BCE when Aristotle's *Poetics* (1961) offered one of the earliest and most famous definitions of the concept. Aristotle also put forward a famous "recipe" for writing tragedies – one that remains influential to this day. Aristotle is often understood to have regarded tragedy as an especially philosophical literary genre. Subsequent interest shown by Hegel, Schopenhauer and Nietzsche, right down to twentieth-century philosophers like Nussbaum and Williams, suggests that there might be something to this belief (Neill 2002). Perhaps its "seriousness" and "magnitude", as Aristotle puts it, are the reasons why so many scholars believe that tragedy can examine and make statements about the human condition more profoundly than any other literary genre.

This inquiry is partly informed by Aristotle, since his definition of tragedy is part of our conceptual backdrop: "Tragedy, then, is an imitation of an action that is serious, complete, and of a certain magnitude, a language embellished with each kind of artistic ornament, the several kinds being found in separate parts of the play; in the form of action, not of narrative; through pity and fear effecting the proper purgation of the emotions" (Aristotle 1961, 61).

In his introduction to *The Poetics* Fergusson explains that by "action", Aristotle does not mean physical activity, deeds or events, but the motives which spur all three in the agent's pursuit of what is regarded as in his or her best interest. Aristotle also describes what he sees as the psychological and hence social value of tragedy: namely the cathartic purging of emotions, especially pity and fear.

In *Wide Sargasso Sea*, Rochester's pursuit of his main motive (wealth) leads to Antoinette's subjection, madness and incarceration, alienation and eventually, even to her death. Antoinette's main motives (happiness and peace) are thwarted. Christophine's hopes (for Antoinette's well-being, and her own) are also unrealized.

Unlike the tragic hero of *Oedipus the King* – Aristotle's model tragedy – Antoinette is not brought down by indomitable forces known to and perhaps controlled only by the gods; her tragedy is the result of human motives, history and social circumstances. Slavery is the big tragedy at the centre of West Indian history. Some scholars have even seen it as Europe's tragedy too. Rhys's novel supports that view. Ironically, it is the abolition of slavery and not slavery itself that directly contributes to the unfolding of Antoinette's tragedy.

Antoinette may not be a tragic hero in all the classical senses of the term, but the fact that she is a heroine, or a "shero" as some would have it, is itself of historical significance. She does, however, share some of the characteristics.

Antoinette experiences a tragic fall, not from being a king to a beggar, like Oedipus, but from being a descendant and heiress of privileged white plantation owners to the tragic circumstances which the novel dramatizes. After belonging to a social class that regards black people as property, she ends up becoming little more than Rochester's property herself. She also falls from the status of being regarded as a normal person to being seen and treated as insane. It is debatable whether death itself is an evil and a tragedy, but few would deny our general horror of the prospect of death. As with many other literary tragedies, this is what Antoinette confronts as she walks with a lit candle along the "dark passage" (Rhys 1997, 124).

We are given no reasons for believing that, like Oedipus and many other traditional tragic heroes, Antoinette is morally noble. Morally, she seems like the ordinary persons, not royalty, who are the focus of modern tragedies. Her fall is due not to the traditional flaw in the hero's character, but to forces in the human heart, and to human imperfectability.

Like some other tragic heroes she does seem to score something of a moral victory at the end by burning down the house of her "owner" and oppressor. She is not altogether a passive victim. She goes down fighting.

It is easy to see how the novel could evoke pity and fear in its readers. Evil, it is said, "is serious unjustified harm inflicted on sentient beings" (Kekes 2000). The harms which befall Antoinette seem to me to be unjustified, and therefore evil. We pity her for this reason. We fear unjustified harm because it can happen to anyone at any time. Sophocles (1965, 149) is aware of this when he ends *Oedipus the King* with these words: "Therefore, while our eyes wait to see the destined final day, we must call no one happy who is of mortal race, until he has crossed life's border, free from pain." This novel, like Aristotle's model tragedy, reminds us of something fundamental in the human condition.

But the novel does not present the recently freed black people and Antoinette as mere passive victims. Both turn to violence, portrayed or suggested, as a way of striking back at their oppressors. And both use the same weapon: fire.

The view that violence is sometimes morally permissible is disturbing to advocates of non-violence, including those who advocate Gandhi's *Satyagraha*. But what are we to make of the two examples of violence in this novel: the burning of Coulibri by the former slaves, and the implied burning of Thornfield Hall by Antoinette?

The former slaves, we are led to believe, hear of Mr Mason's plan to import labourers from the East Indies to work on Coulibri Estate. This will reduce or even eliminate employment opportunities for them. Having endured the inhumanity and injustice of slavery, they are about to be struck another blow. So they rebel in anger and retaliate. The right to rebel against oppressive conditions is now upheld by virtually all philosophers, even if they disagree on the morally permissible means of doing so. Theoretically the blacks have other means at their disposal: protest, negotiation, moral suasion and so on. But given the failed pacifism of Sam Sharpe in Jamaica – to give a real life example – it is doubtful that these would be viable options in these historical circumstances.

The mad woman in *Jane Eyre* succeeds in burning down Thornfield Hall. In Rhys's novel, before Antoinette heads for the dark passage with the lit candle, she has a moment of illumination: "Now at last I know why I was brought here and what I have to do" (Rhys 1997, 124). Given the links between the two novels, it seems reasonable to infer that Rhys intends results similar to *Jane Eyre's* or is at least open to its possibility.

Earlier I said that the position which interpreters take on the question of whether or not Antoinette would be morally responsible for her arson will influence the meaning they give to the novel. If her arson is the irrational act of a deranged person, then this is a disaster novel. If it is an intentional and rational act, then it is a protest novel. I believe it is the latter. We are not given the embodiment of Antoinette's reasoning in the form of an argument, but if a narrative can be as persuasive as an argument – and I believe it can be – then her story has the force of a piece of practical reasoning: it tells her what she has to do and why. In *Jane Eyre* the burning is a "dreadful calamity" brought about by a lunatic (Brontë 1959, 520–21). In Rhys's novel it becomes the moral retribution of a deeply injured woman.

Neither the burning of Coulibri nor the burning of Thornfield Hall will advance the material self-interest of those who start the fires: the former slaves may even be worse off economically, and Antoinette will be dead. Both cases seem to be instances of the mystical and therapeutic violence which some interpreters discern in Fanon (1963). It is the kind of violence which its advocates associate with expressive, communicative or even spiritual value. For Rhys, the fire is probably a symbol of cleansing much as it is for some reggae musicians.

I will conclude with some remarks on the relation between the form of the novel and its author's view on how we ought to live. The story is told through a sequence of first-person narratives. The obvious philosophical aspect of this technique is its respect for the autonomy of the characters. They speak for themselves, and this includes the oppressor and the victim. If Antoinette is intended to be mad, she is taken out of the silence which Foucault describes, and given a voice which was once denied such persons. Autonomy is a central concept in both moral and political philosophy. It is a key principle in Kantian and applied ethics. In both its moral and political uses, it is linked to self-determination and sovereignty over oneself. The denial and suppression of autonomy is at the centre of the tragic vision of *Wide Sargasso Sea.*

Chapter 7

African Conceptions of a Person and *Myal*

African philosophy includes ancient Egyptian writings, aspects of Arabic philosophy, seventeenth-century Ethiopian thought, the so-called ethnophilosophy of the societies which lacked strong scribal traditions, as well as the work of modern philosophers educated in the universities which European colonizers introduced to the Continent. Its concerns include the study of traditional African thought, comparison with other, especially Western, systems of thought, the decolonization of concepts of Africa, the political thought of its major leaders, and pressing questions such as the role of violence and democracy in African life. Work is also being done in virtually all the core areas of philosophy, including metaphysics, logic, epistemology, ethics, aesthetics and the philosophy of religion (Wiredu 2004).

Among its concerns is the question: What is a person? This is one of the central questions of philosophy everywhere. For more than two thousand years Western philosophers have argued that human beings are made of an immaterial mind or soul – the words are often used interchangeably – linked to a material body. Plato and Descartes are two of the philosophers most associated with this view. Few contemporary philosophers hold this view of the person. But it is the view probably most widely held by the man in the street. Many Africans, as we shall see, hold very different conceptions.

Kaphagawani offers a survey of research on conceptions of persons held by the Akan and Yoruba of West Africa, and the Bantu of East and Southern Africa. He quotes Wiredu's claim that the Akan have a tripartite conception of the person consisting of "*nipadua*" (body), *okra* (life-giving entity) and *sunsum* (that which gives a person personality") (Kaphagawani 2004, 332). There has been considerable controversy, especially between Wiredu and Gyekye, over the question of whether or not the term *okra* should be translated as the Western "soul". There is a similar dispute over the alleged immateriality, immortality and divinity of the *sunsum*.

He cites Ghadegesin's claim that the Yoruba view a person as consisting of "four elements: the *ara, okan, emi* and *ori*" (p. 334). The *ara* is the physical part of the body. The *okan* is dualistically conceived as both the physical cause of the circulation of the blood and the seat of psychic and emotional reactions. Ghadegesin also claims that the *emi* is "the active principle of life, the life-giving element put in place by the deity" (ibid.). The *ori* is also dualistically conceived as being the human head as well as the determinant of the person's personality and the bearer of his fate. There is much debate over the alleged immateriality and independence of the *emi*.

Kaphagawani also examines Tempels's thesis that the Bantu view a person as a force rather than as a static object, and he considers Mbiti's account of their sociocentric view of the formation of a person. In this view it is the community or society that produces personhood, and it is summed up in the saying, "I am, because we are; and since we are therefore I am" (quoted in Kaphagawani 2004, 337). He also quotes Kagame's account of his shadow thesis, their view that a person is made of "the vital principle of animality known as shadow", but who, at the same time, "is animated by a second vital principle which is immortal and in which are anchored the intelligent operations proper to man" (p. 339).

It is not at all clear, Kaphagawani admits, what Kagame means by "shadow". It may be a metaphorical reference to the absence of personality at death, for the Bantu believe that the union between the shadow and the intelligence is dissolved at death, and that the shadow disappears. Of interest too is Wiredu's claim that the Akan word *sunsum* literally means "shadow".

Wiredu (2004) believes that communitarianism and normativity are the two aspects of personhood which are most important in traditional African thought. Ghadegesin also claims that normativity, the learning of values, is an important part of the Yoruba conception of personhood. Menkiti (2004) has studied its role in the African conception of human destiny. Masolo (2004) also takes African comunitarianism seriously, and compares it with Western views.

In this chapter I wish to argue that Erna Brodber, in her novel *Myal* (1988), follows the African tradition in stressing the communitarian and normative aspects of personhood. I shall also try to show that her educational philosophy is linked to both.

According to Wiredu, the normative (ethical) aspects of the African conceptions of personhood have attracted much more attention than their metaphysical dimensions. But as Murdoch (1992) reminds us, metaphysics can be a guide to morals, and I might add, to political and educational philosophy as well. So before moving on to these issues, it is important to clarify some of the metaphysical assumptions on which these aspects of the novel are based.

Myal, the Jamaican religion from which the novel gets its title, can be traced back to the 1760s, according to Schuler (1979). It began as an attempt by the slaves to protect themselves from European sorcery. Later, the religion directed its anti-sorcery campaign against obeah, which is Jamaican sorcery. Some writers see this as a survival of the African belief that all evils, including illness, are caused by sorcery. Warner-Lewis (2003) suggests that the word "myal" may be derived from an African word "mayaala" which denotes someone who represents the power of God, spirits or ancestors. It gradually became an Afro-Christian religion – like the Antoine movement in Africa, Warner-Lewis suggests – and Myalists came to see themselves as agents of God fighting against obeah, the cause of all personal and social evils.

The Jamaican conception of personhood, especially as it is found in the country's folk culture, is in need of study. This is foundational to all of the country's religions, including indigenous ones like Kumina and Revivalism, which seem to have emerged out of Myal. Here I shall focus on Brodber's perception of it, first in one of her non-fiction works, and then in *Myal*.

"Most West African societies," she writes, "had a notion of man as a duality, having a tangible self and another sometimes called the shadow" (Brodber 2003, 64). Brodber describes the shadow as an invisible entity, and she refers to *Obeye*, a special God-given power which was used to exact secret vengeance. Brodber sees this as the African origin of obeah.

It is not clear whether Brodber regards shadow and *Obeye* as one and the same. Senior (2003, 341) reports that in the nineteenth century, obeah practitioners were seen as "shadow-takers", people capable of stealing other people's souls and causing them various evils, including illness and death. According to her, the spirits called duppies by Jamaicans (murder is called duppy-making) are seen as the shadow dimension of the person. In the Kumina religion, she claims, it is believed that one possesses two souls: a spirit which goes to God after death and may become an ancestral spirit and return to earth; and the shadow which may remain in the grave, but can also choose to leave, or be summoned and directed by the obeah practitioner.

Brodber sees obeah as part of the justice system in a society where people distrusted courts, had little knowledge of them, or lived too far away. Obeah is secretive, involving arrangements between the client and the practitioner. Since it could wreak social havoc, especially when performed by tricksters, it was eventually made illegal.

According to Brodber, Myal arose as an antidote to obeah. In her view, the new religion combined positive aspects of African witchcraft with Christianity in what could be called the freedman's creolized response to his situation. Unlike obeah it was public. Myalists marched to cotton trees to pull out the obeah which its practitioners had buried there. They engaged in drumming and spirit possession. Their movement was communitarian rather than individualistic.

Both Senior (2003) and Wilkins (1988) emphasize the role that Myal played in the medical history of Jamaica. The belief that illness can be caused by an obeah, practitioner stealing a person's spirit, or by directing the spirits of others, apparently still exists in Jamaica. So does the belief that Myalists can restore souls and health.

It is clear that the Bantu and apparently Akan belief that the shadow is part of a person has survived in Jamaica. There could be similarities between the tripartite view of the person found in Kumina and that of the Akan, but this is not altogether clear. It could be that the concepts have been creolized. Brodber's account of the African concept of a person strongly resembles Western dualism, except for the obeah applications. (I am not aware of similar applications in Western sorcery.) Perhaps notions like the *sunsum* and the *emi* have their equivalents or derivations in Jamaican folk thought. But the shadow thesis, as Kaphagawani calls it, seems as mysterious in Jamaica as it is in Africa. For one thing, the Jamaican version of the shadow seems to resemble the Western notion of soul or spirit. Only further anthropological and philosophical work can untangle these matters. But this is not our concern here.

What is important is that Brodber seems to have taken from obeah the notion of spirit theft. And from Myal she has taken the notion of spiritual healing through the restoration of spirits. I shall argue that she integrates these metaphysical notions into a form of communitarianism, an existential ethical norm, and an educational philosophy.

It might be helpful to state these assumptions more clearly. I think the novel rests on the following six presuppositions:

1. A human person is made of a body and spirit (shadow).
2. This spirit can be stolen.
3. A stolen spirit results in illness or illfare (the opposite of welfare), a term used by some Buddhists.
4. A spirit can be restored by persons with the power to do so.
5. Restoration of the spirit results in wellness.
6. A society is analogous to a person; it is a person writ large, as Plato would say.

Before proceeding to Brodber's use of these notions in the novel, we should note some of its explicitly stated conceptions of personhood. Anita's studying is described as "the kind that splits the mind from the body and both from the soul and leaves each open to infiltration" (Brodber 1988, 28). This resembles the New Age tripartite view of the person. The following description of Ella suggests Western dualism: "And even her mind came into the act. It was now struggling for a balance with her body" (p. 80). A similar dualism is expressed in William Brassington's view of his wife as "one whose spirit had, as it were, grown a body which was housed like a spare part in the body he knew" (p. 90). Reverend Simpson also describes zombification in places like Africa, Haiti and Brazil in a dualistic fashion: "People are separated from the parts of themselves that make them think and they are left as flesh only. Flesh that takes directions from someone. The thinking part of them is also used as nefariously . . . 'immorally' might be a better word" (p. 108).

At the heart of *Myal* there is a developing dialectic between spirit thieves and spirit restorers. It is, obviously, also a dialectic between evil and good. I shall now examine how this dialectic is played out.

The most literal of the spirit thieves is Mass Levi. A former district constable and a successful farmer, he is portrayed as a much admired man.

His economic success enables him to lend money to others, and he even has his own privy. His children are also successful and they bask in his fame. Although he is attractive to women, he is faithful to his wife. But he has one dark secret which is known only to himself and his wife. He is impotent. He tries to restore his potency by using obeah to steal the spirit of Anita, an attractive and bright teenager. His obeah seems to result in paranormal events like the poltergeist's stoning of the girl's home, and strange, unusual visitations in her bed. While performing an obeah ritual in his privy – which is secretly observed by his wife – he dies.

Anita's spirit is restored by Miss Gatha, a Kumina leader. On 27 January she chants, "Nine times three is twenty-seven. Three times three times three" (p. 71). Dressed in ritual garments of red and white, Miss Gatha and the visitors to her tabernacle use singing and drumming to help her into the spirit. During her spiritual ecstasy, Miss Gatha's face alternates between that of a fifteen-year-old girl and that of a woman closer to her actual age (more than sixty years old). She manages to restore Anita's spirit: "She blew again, said softly 'It is finished,' and with that all took what they had and left Miss Gatha's form with its fifteen-year-old face on the ground" (p. 73).

William Brassington, the Methodist parson, is also a spirit thief. A mulatto who was educated in England, his motto is "to exorcise and replace". His wife Maydene accuses him: "William, you are a spirit thief" (p. 18). She also describes his perception of his ministry: "Humility. My people have a far way to go and a far way we can go but we must understand how far back we are and submit so that we can learn" (p. 21).

His English-born wife, Maydene, plays an important role in the restoration of his own spirit, as well as that of the community. According to the narrator, "Maydene saw herself as the monitor of her husband's soul" (p. 14). She goes for long walks, especially at nightfall, in the community of Grove Town in St Thomas, where most of the novel is set, and gets to know the local people. She cannot understand why Miss Gatha should not wear her head-tie, instead of a hat in church. Emphasizing the pedagogic dictum that the teacher should go from the known to the unknown, she believes it would be better if her husband tried to link what the people already know to what he wanted them to learn. Regarded as spiritually strange by her husband, she forms an important bond with Miss Gatha. She also influences her husband's collaboration with Reverend Simpson, the black-conscious Baptist parson whom she regards as a very spiritually evolved man. Maydene is the first to regard Ella's illness as the result of spirit theft, and she plays a leading role in the communitarian healing ritual which will be discussed later.

The educational system is also portrayed as a primary instrument of spirit theft. The reader may already know some of the relevant historical background. In his account of the development of literature as a discipline, Culler (1997, 35–36) writes: "In nineteenth-century England, literature emerged as an extremely important idea, a special kind of writing charged with several functions. Made a subject of instruction in the colonies of the British Empire, it was charged with giving the natives an appreciation of the greatness of England and engaging them as grateful participants in a historic civilizing enterprise."

In *Myal*, set in the early twentieth century, we see Ella, a thirteen-year-old mixed race girl, reciting Rudyard Kipling's poetry, including the famous (infamous?) line "Take up the whiteman's burden" (Brodber 1988, 6). The poem is seen by the educators as an excellent way of teaching history, geography, civics and a love of the Empire. Ella's performance amazes and delights the Anglican parson and teacher Holness. But Reverend Simpson is disturbed by what he sees and hears. He will later play an important role in the restoration of spirits in the novel, as well as in the articulation of its educational philosophy.

When Ella grows up and becomes a teacher in the community, she is dissatisfied with the message in the textbook she is required to teach (some readers will recognize it as *Caribbean Reader*). She is especially disturbed by a farmyard fable which tells of oppressed animals who rebel and leave the farm, but who eventually return to be cared for. Ella believes it is natural for animals to live without masters. She believes that the author of the text "has robbed his characters of their possibilities" (p. 106). Even the Reverend William Brassington comes to see it as a "negative lesson" (p. 103).

Mainly through dialogue with Reverend Simpson, Ella develops a libertarian educational philosophy of her own. This method is reminiscent of the dialogics which Paulo Freire (2003, 8) sees as "the essence of education as the practice of freedom". Simpson, in what appears to be an imaginary conversation with Ole African, sees the text's educational strategy as the embodiment of the two main principles of spirit theft: make them believe there is nowhere to go, and make them believe that their brightest are their dumbest. The book aims at zombification, for the author has "taken their knowledge of their original and natural world away from them and left them empty shells – duppies, zombies, living deads capable only of receiving orders from someone else and carrying them out" (Brodber 1988, 107). As a Baptist parson – the Baptists historically influenced Myal – Simpson is portrayed as a man who understands that there are many different kinds of knowledge. He sings a Negro Spiritual about the liberation of his people. He is respected by Miss Gatha and Ole African. He quotes Bible verses about spiritual freedom and power. In his role as a spirit restorer, he offers Ella this bit of educational advice: "He wrote, you think without an awareness of certain things. But does he force you to teach without this awareness? Need your voice say what his says?" (ibid.). Freire would call this critical consciousness. Maxine Greene (1973, 7) would see it as a core activity in educational philosophy. It is an educational strategy to be used to restore the spirit stolen by colonial ideology.

In Reverend Simpson's view, this educational philosophy will help to bring about the social transformation which he envisages: "We have people who can and are willing to correct images from the inside, destroy what should be destroyed, replace it with what it should be replaced and put us back together, give us back ourselves with which to chart our course to go where we want to go" (Brodber 1988, 110). The normally reticent Miss Gatha, in a poem, begs the rogues of Whitehall to change their tune and allow the society a style which is consistent with both its time and clime (p. 111).

Selwyn Langley, Ella's American husband, is arguably the major individual spirit thief in the novel. A descendant of a long line of manufacturers of herbal medicines, he is, ironically, the cause of Ella's illness. While she is living with him in Baltimore, Ella's childhood fantasy world of characters like Peter Pan, Dairy Maid and Lucy Gray become her lived reality. They come to occupy the uppermost part of her mind while the people of Grove Town sink to the bottom.

Langley rejects his family tradition in favour of show business. *Caribbean Nights and Days*, the play that he writes and stages, is inspired by Ella and her world. But when she sees it, Ella is shocked and disturbed. While it contains some superficial similarities to her Caribbean world, it is clearly the work of a writer who "knew nothing about Easter as star-apple time and midsummer for mangoes and of summer the breadfruit season" (p. 83) In the American tradition of the time, it is a coon show. Langley also wants to make it into a film which would trap the spirit of Grove Town for future ages. Ella describes his spirit theft as follows: "He took everything I had away. Made what he wanted of it and gave me back nothing" (p. 84).

Langley does not want his fellow Americans to know that his wife is a mulatto, so he concocts a fictional biography for them. Ella wants to have a child, but her husband fears miscegenation and so resorts to prophylactics and onanism. As a result Ella becomes very ill with "a bad bad water belly" (p. 96). They are unable to find a cure in America, so she is sent back to Jamaica.

A cure is effected by Mass Cyrus, a Myal man. In the African tradition, he recognizes that Ella's illness has a spiritual cause – spirit theft – and so requires a more difficult cure than those administered for bodily illnesses. In fact, the cure is so difficult and serious that it sets off another of the novel's paranormal events, a hurricane: "all this sudden destruction because Ella O'Grady-Langley lying still like a Grecian sacrifice upon a pyre had gone too far, had tripped out in foreign" (p. 4). But Mass Cyrus sets out to touch the peace within her and succeeds.

It is significant that although led by Mass Cyrus, the Myal ritual is conducted by members of the community representing different races, classes and genders. In the African tradition of communitarianism, it is the Grove Town community which guides Ella to self-formation, and to the healing cultivation of her personhood.

Communitarianism is an important movement in contemporary political philosophy. Kymlicka (1993) sees it as the completion of the French Revolution's ideals of liberty, equality and fraternity. In his view, it lacks the futuristic hope of Marxist communism, and seeks instead to preserve and emphasize whatever communalism already exists in a society.

Masolo (2004) argues that while in the West communitarianism arose primarily as a critique of individualistic liberalism – with origins at least as far back as Hegel – African communitarianism, by contrast, is strongly prescriptive. The tension between individual and community rights raises important philosophical questions for both traditions, but these need not concern us here.

Brodber's communitarianism is evident even in her literary techniques. O'Callaghan (1998, 236) points out that there is no dominant narrator's voice in the novel. The stories are told by a community of voices. According to her, "the communal voice implies a wide range of discursive techniques. We are treated to anecdotes, songs and spells, statistics, dreams and lyrical fantasies, tongue-in-cheek pronouncements, puns, cozy, practical wisdom, schoolbook stories and parables." It is also true that the novel does not focus on the story of a single character, but on the stories of the members of a community.

Communities, of course, operate according to their normative ideals. Menkiti (2004, 326) claims that the African conception of a person is normative in the sense that it views personhood as a stage of "moral arrival". It is achieved when someone reaches a certain level of moral functioning. It appears that such a view can be found in many African societies.

What Ella and some of the other characters in the novel achieve is, I think, something akin to the Existentialist notion of authenticity. The major philosophers in this tradition differ in their conceptions of it. I am using the term in its Sartrean sense: to avoid bad faith by accepting the freedom to take control of one's existence, and to thereby release the power to live a fulfilling life in accordance with one's true nature. This is the foundation of Existentialist ethics in the sense that this view commits its adherents to treating others in such a way that they too enjoy the freedom to live authentically (Cooper 2000). I suggest that this conception is, for Ella, the equivalent of the moral arrival that Menkiti describes.

Ella's quarrel with the fable in the textbook is that it denies the animals the freedom to live authentically. Her conversation with Reverend Simpson makes her realize that her own authenticity has been achieved through the Myalian cure of her zombification. Her educational philosophy tries to facilitate the development of similar authenticity in her students and her society. It is widely thought that the idea of moral value is built into the concept of education, insofar as it is seen as a moral good. The view here, apparently, is that the aim of personhood, as well as education, is to live authentically.

It seems reasonable to suppose that there are reasons why Brodber chooses to give a mixed race girl of African, Irish and perhaps Moorish, descent a central place in the design of her novel. American literature, it will be noted, is full of what Zack (1993, 140) calls "genocidal images of mixed race" which result from a binary conception of race. Patterson (2004, 647), observes that multiculturalism is undermining this mindset and he points out that "nonbinary racial classification is the norm among the vast majority of non-European peoples".

Maydene's father, an amateur anthropologist, sees brownness as the origin and destiny of mankind. He believes it explains the greatness

African Conceptions of a Person and *Myal*

of Pushkin and Beethoven. Mass Cyrus regards Ella as a new kind of "in-between colours" and "trained-minded people" who are out of tune with the rest of the society, and who therefore bring "pain, confusion and destruction" to themselves and others (Brodber 1988, 1–3). Life is hard for Ella growing up in a predominantly black society. Other children call her nicknames like "Salt pork", "Alabaster baby" and "Red Ants Abundance" (p. 9). Although they themselves are probably infected, they refuse to sit beside her, alleging that she has lice. The teachers, too, ignore her, believing that in the colour-stratified pyramid of the society, she will probably succeed without their help.

But Maydene sees similarities between Ella's suffering and the experiences of her husband. Because of their colour, they are alienated from the rest of the society. Maydene and her husband arrange to adopt Ella and to give her the opportunity to get an education.

There are aspects of the tragic mulatto theme, but ultimately, I think, the novel rejects a genocidal attitude to its mixed race characters. It emphasizes community rather than race. O'Callaghan sees Ella as an embodiment of the Jamaican motto: Out of Many, One People. The Myal religion is a creolized cultural phenomenon; it is not exclusively a racial one. I think Brodber uses Myalian healing as a metaphor for cultural well-being and wholeness.

That Brodber intends an African dimension to the development of personhood in this Jamaican community is also evident in the character of Ole African. He is a spirit who appears in the form of a scarecrow-as-crucifix at the poltergeist's house. When he appears to Ella and Maydene, also as a scarecrow, he reminds Maydene of an African stiltman. He also appears to Reverend Simpson in a dream, and tells him how to defeat the spirit thieves and how to use the colonizer's books to help the community find its way back home. Like Diogenes, the ancient Greek philosopher who lived in a barrel, Ole African is a philosopher who appears to his descendants dressed in dirty old clothes which look like strips of leather. His philosophy is summed up in his well-known slogan: "The half has never been told."

His mission, it appears, is to tell the African half of the story. Although all the children in the community have known and heard about him for centuries as the great punisher, Ella, in response to Maydene's question at the sighting, denies that she knows him, in words echoing Peter's denial of Jesus in the Bible. The rectification of Ella's denial and the affirmation of the African dimension of personhood are clearly part of the aims of the novel.

Chapter 8

The Law of Karma in *Sastra*

The Indian philosophical tradition is among the oldest in the world. According to Mohanty (1993, 334 and xxxvi), it is distinguished by its own "concerns, questions, goals, style, rhetoric", and has its own exhilarating "aesthetic perfume". Hamilton (2001) reminds us that although philosophy and religion are pursued separately in the West, especially since Kant, this is not the case in India. There philosophy is seen as the quest for an understanding of the nature of reality, as an accompaniment to the religious goal of personal salvation. The two traditions work closely together in India's great religions which include Hinduism, Buddhism and Jainism.

Many writers argue that belief in karma and rebirth are the twin philosophical foundations of Indian civilization. Whether or not this is true, their pervasiveness in Indian thought cannot be denied. Since my main focus here is on karma, a brief account of this concept may be helpful.

Belief in this "action-consequence mechanism", as Hamilton (2001, 12) calls it, is rooted in the philosophically important concept of causation. She argues that the concept of karma emerged from the belief that the functioning of the universe could be influenced by sacrificial rituals. In time it was believed that these actions not only influenced the cosmos, but also benefited those who performed them. Since effects follow causes (at least in the world we know), this led to the view that all actions have retributive powers that extend into the future, even beyond death; this belief, it is said, in turn gave rise to the concept of rebirth. By stressing that intentions are the most important actions of all, Siddartha Gotama, the Buddha, added a moral dimension to the concept of karma. The view developed that causation is at work not only in the material universe, but in the moral and spiritual dimensions as well. Bilimoria (1993) points out that it also came to be linked to the idea of justice: merit requires future reward; demerit, future punishment. Karma, then, is the view that our actions, including decisions and choices, will determine the kinds of persons we become in the future, as well as the things which will happen to us. The lives we are living now were determined by our past actions. This worldview led one Indian pundit to describe the 2004 tsunami as the release of a large quantity of man-made evil that had been pent up on the earth. In Indian thought, karma has the status of a natural law.

Billington (1997) distinguishes between three types of karma: (1) *prarabda-karma* – the consequences of actions in a previous existence which work themselves out in this life; (2) *sanchita-karma* – consequences of past actions which will affect a future life; and (3) *agami-karma* – consequences which affect the present. We are powerless to influence (1) and (2), but we can do something about (3).

Some writers regard karma as a variant of Indian fatalism (Woods 2000). I take fatalism to be the view that whatever happens is inevitable. It may be the acceptance of hard determinism and a complete denial of human freedom. Or it may be an attitude of mind, a resigned acceptance of whatever happens in life.

It is easy to see how from the agent's point of view, *prarabda-karma* and *sanchita-karma* may be regarded as fatalistic; he or she can do nothing about them, so resigned acceptance seems the prudent option. But it was *agami-karma* which set them in motion in the first place, and this is based on free will. So all three forms of karma are really examples of free will in action. Billington (1997, 39) quotes Nehru's way of conceptualizing this philosophical issue: "It's like a game of cards: determinism is the hand you're dealt: free will is how you play it."

Like all philosophic-religious concepts, karma has psychological and social functions. It gives people a way of interpreting and coping with their experiences. Halbfass (2000) points out that it provides an explanation for the things that happen in life; if, for example, it is true, then there are no accidents of birth (Bilimoria 1993), and perhaps no accidents at all. It is also a reason for both religious and moral discipline. It also provides a rationale for wanting to be liberated from the material world.

When Indians began arriving in the West Indies as indentured labourers after the abolition of slavery in the nineteenth century, they brought the concepts of karma and rebirth with them. Finding themselves in a New World and more cosmopolitan society, many have clung tenaciously to their traditional Indian culture. But some accommodation with the West was inevitable, and this gave way to various forms of West Indian creolization, as well as engagement with a wider world.

In her novel *Sastra* (1993), Lakshmi Persaud portrays characters in a Hindu community in Trinidad in the 1950s. An Indian woman writing about experiences of women in the Caribbean appears to be a recent development (Salick 1986; Mehta 2004). At the heart of this novel is one of the central questions in the philosophical study of multiculturalism: How is culture related to the well-being of individuals? The novel is about Sastra, a young woman who confronts a major conflict in her late adolescence and early womanhood. Her parents and others close to her believe that obedience to their traditional culture is in her best interest, and that she should therefore marry Govind, the young man chosen for her by the elders. But she is in love with Rabindranath who has less going for him. She must choose between the claims of traditional wisdom made on the one hand, and the influences of Western liberal notions like individual freedom and self-determination on the other.

My main focus will be on the role played by the concept of karma in this account of a process of cultural conflict and accommodation. Attention will be paid to different views of it within the community portrayed. I shall also focus on the dynamics of the interaction between Hindu traditionalism and Western liberalism and cosmopolitanism.

The novel opens with Parvatee Narayan's visit to Pundit Karsi for a reading of her child's karma or destiny. The pundit explains that the Sanskrit scriptures, believed to be the words of the gods, reveal that the child has two reincarnations instead of the usual one. According to the first, "if Sastra keeps to the traditional path of honour, dignity, womanhood; if she keeps to the heart of her culture, her life will be secure, content like her sister's" (Persaud 1993, 9). The pundit foresees misery if she chooses self over family and follows someone who wants to teach her how to fly. He prudently does not spell out the alternative that he sees: "a period of violent upheaval would come to pass – those years between the death and birth of reincarnations – persons close to the child would be gravely inflicted by intense pain and deep sorrow . . . the faith of one and the life of another would be severely handicapped . . . such close juxtapositions of death and life ever brought turmoil – violence explosions, upheavals of the earth and sun – Tsunami" (pp. 10–11).

Divine prediction or the patriarchal control of women? Mehta (2004) seems to think it is the second. In any case, Parvatee takes these predictions to heart and believes "that fate had spun a web of singing, dancing light, chased by chained ghosts from the underworld" (Persaud 1993, 15). In believing the pundit's predictions Parvatee seems to exemplify the widely held view that women are the main bearers of custom and tradition in a society.

But her husband Narayan is a sceptic. He believes in the power of the mind and will to determine a person's destiny. He sees karma as "the refuge of those unable or unwilling to better their lives, seeking solace" (p. 215). He believes in the force and immediacy of the present. Pundit Karsi is aware of Narayan's beliefs and sees merit in them: they make people try harder. But he is deeply convinced of the power of the action-reaction mechanism in the interconnectedness of all things. He thinks that just as the ocean is pulled by the sun and moon, similarly, there are other forces apart from ourselves which determine our destiny.

The novel presents a tension between Parvatee's belief in the traditional philosophy and what the narrator calls Narayan's philosophy of hope.

In the Hindu community of which Sastra is a part, people's lives are also governed by belief in another important Indian philosophical concept: dharma. Shakuntala Tiwari, Govind's mother, sees it as "the path of righteousness, the way of life handed down by teaching and example, from her parents and grandparents, to her and her son" (p. 37). The narrator also describes an ethical objectivist point of view which sees it as Truth, or the divine rules and values that people should live by. Bilmoria says it "gives an overall form to a system of positive law, mores and regulations which are cultural imperatives, the contents of which are determined by various factors, more particularly the voice of tradition, convention or custom and the conscience of the learned" (1993, 46). Dharma is a way of easing the burden of karma.

As a learned man, and a man of conscience, Pundit Karsi is a part of dharma. So is the conventional belief that parents are more experienced and wiser than their children, and therefore more qualified to decide whom they should marry. It is dharma in action when Sastra's parents and Govind's parents decide that Sastra and Govind should be married.

But Sastra, now in her late teens, discovers that Rabindranath, her slightly older former teacher, is in love with her. Rabindranath is a Christian since his father Surinder converted, it is believed, in order to become the headmaster of a school run by the Presbyterians. Rabindranath is a dedicated teacher who serves his community by teaching the College Exhibition class. He encourages Sastra to read Tolstoy's *Anna Karenina*, a novel about lovers going against social convention, which he views as a reflection of their own situation, and as a cautionary tale advocating reason above the passions – the position he advises her to take. He also believes that her accomplishment as an educated woman should influence her decision about marriage.

Rabindranath's commitment to reason is reflected in his decision to study mathematics and philosophy – subjects widely associated with reason and rationality. He and Sastra also have philosophical discussions about such matters as the alleged continuum between the physical and the spiritual.

Rabindranath is also an egalitarian nationalist and something of a humanist. The death by fire of an Indian money-lender and his family leads some members of the Indian community to conclude that it is an act of murder committed by African Trinidadians. In an ensuing discussion of Indo-African relations in Trinidad – another important issue which the novel addresses – Rabindranath gives his views on this topic. He rejects the Indian stereotype of African Trinidadians as irresponsible carnival-loving hedonists. He sees their carnival as a celebration of freedom from the injustices, contempt, hostility and cultural suppression they experienced under slavery. He admires their courage and faith, and finds in them the same warmth, sensitivity and generosity that he finds in his own people. Differences between people, he believes, are superficial: "It is our common humanity that matters. What is the shape of the human spirit? What is the colour of human courage?" (Persaud 1993, 83). The two groups are inseparably linked, he claims, and he argues for national unity. He is dismissed as an idealist who has spent too much time with books and children.

Govind, his rival, seems to have everything going for him: religion, caste, wealth, good looks, character, personality, intelligence, profession (he plans to become a doctor) and close ties of friendship with Sastra's family. The karmic predictions also favour him.

The difficult choice facing Sastra may be described as follows: If she chooses Rabindranath she will be a first-timer, breaking with her family's Hindu tradition and making a choice which will cause much grief, disappointment and unhappiness within the family. Yet he is urging her to fly, and when she is with him she feels as if she is "sailing in the sky" (p. 102). She is also afraid to love, for she remembers Dolly, the unmarried pregnant girl abandoned by her father, and by the father of her unborn child. Dolly also appears as a suicide in Sastra's dream, and warns her against love.

If she chooses Govind, she will be acting in accordance with both traditional wisdom and the apparent dictates of reason. In strict utilitarian terms, this choice would bring about the greatest happiness for the greatest number. But the wedding would only be a dutiful, honourable, traditional family ceremony.

When Rabindranath becomes ill, at the school's request Sastra takes over his College Exhibition class. They have daily meetings as he guides her teaching from his home. They become even closer as she shares his commitment to his pupils and his community.

Sastra resists pressures from her elders for an early engagement to Govind. She decides to put her career first. She goes to Ireland to further her studies. Rabindranath and Govind go to England for their higher education.

While in Ireland Sastra writes several letters to Rabindranath but he does not reply. When she completes her studies and returns to Trinidad she discovers the reason for his silence. He has leukaemia and has been given only a few years to live.

For Govind's backers this is another reason why Rabindranath and Sastra should not get married. Rabindranath, too, sees the merit of their position: "On seeing this, Reason, the faculty he long revered, stood up and said, 'You must know it cannot be right to marry and leave her disadvantaged for far more years than your lives together will be'" (p. 212). He, like Narayan, is very aware that a Hindu widow with children has very little chance of re-marriage.

But Sastra decides that this is a price she is willing to pay for what she wants. She will no longer allow thought, reason and custom to tie her feet. She says to Rabindranath: "I do not wish to listen to reason; it is dull and is without passion. It has been my close companion for too long" (p. 208).

She pleads with Rabindranath: "Stir my soul and let my spirit fly. Help me, Rabindranath, to sing and dance and shout and laugh" (p. 209). She refuses to mould "her inner feelings to a traditional design" (p. 213).

Govind's mother, Shakuntala, is shocked by this desire for self-gratification. She disapprovingly regards the self as the gasoline on which the modern world runs. Her experience has taught her that if one is lucky, "quiet satisfaction" is the most that one can expect from life (p. 157). For Sastra's father, Narayan, "Life is not about idealism. It is about judgment, about seeing a situation, assessing it and doing the best under the circumstances" (p. 215).

But the two lovers want nothing short of a mystical transformation of consciousness. According to Sastra, "My marriage to Rabindranath would transform my life into a beautiful, translucent thing, not an ordinary thing" (ibid.). For her, Rabindranath is the man who found her lost slipper at the river and returned it, completing the pair. This has become a symbol of their union. According to Rabindranath: "My sole reason for wishing to marry her is that my life would become a joyous thing, not an existence" (p. 216). They want their lives to become what Milly will later describe as a "life together like beautiful music; it is the meaning of being" (p. 242). Rabindranath's confrontation with death has intensified his appreciation of life, causing him to view the rest of his days as fine liquor to be sipped and enjoyed as its level sinks in the cask.

The novel echoes Hume's belief that "Reason is and ought only to be the slave of the passions, and can never pretend to any other office than to serve and obey them" (quoted in Ayer 1980, 80). It is also in keeping with the view held by the protagonist of Dostoevsky's philosophical novel *Notes from Underground* (1993, 28): "I, for example, quite naturally want to live so as to satisfy my whole capacity for living, and not so as to satisfy just my reasoning capacity alone, which is some twentieth part of my whole capacity for living." Some would no doubt think that the Underground Man is generous in the extent to which he thinks man is a rational animal. Some will prefer Nietzsche's view that there is a quantity of reason in every passion, and that the emotions have a logic of their own. Consistent with Hume's dictum, Sastra and Rabindranath proceed to put reason in the service of their passions; and like the Underground Man, they decide to cater to their larger "capacity for living".

They have a modest family wedding with Hindu rituals, but without the usual artistry and music. They have a son and a daughter. Rabindranath dies in his wife's arms, shortly after telling her that she was the joy of his life.

Reason also leads to Sastra's migration to Canada. Mehta (2004, 29) sees this as "a postcolonial *kala pani* crossing to North America in search of a recuperated self that transgresses confinement through immigration". I suggest that, more specifically, it is a choice in favour of cosmopolitanism and liberalism. In Toronto, Sastra finds herself in the company of immigrants from other countries and cultures. Most importantly, she is in a culture which nurtures the freedom to choose, something she can no longer imagine living without.

In Toronto, she buries Dr Lal, a close acquaintance in Trinidad, who, after not following his heart and courting Sati, her sister, becomes a lonely and disappointed man. Govind is left behind in Trinidad. He is married to a fellow doctor, but their chain-smoking suggests anxiety and discontent.

Sastra's journey to multi-ethnic Toronto is one aspect of the novel's cosmopolitanism. The other is embodied in Milly, the black housekeeper who Rabindranath inherits from his father Surinder. Born in Barbados where her Aunt Jenny advised her to walk the entire earth, she lives and works in Trinidad, migrates to Boston after Rabindranath's death, and marries a St Lucian. Her cosmopolitanism is encouraged by Surinder, himself a Hindu-turned-Christian, who advises her to be like a bird and enjoy all the cultural forests of the world. She masters Indian cooking after being taught by an expert.

She warns her nephew Francis against the anti-Indian sentiments of his friend Carl Munroe, who is something of an Afro-West Indian cultural nationalist, whose interests are focused mainly on things like the

Shango religion and steelband music. Francis accuses her of being Indi-anized, and of no longer identifying with her race. She replies that Afri-cans had to grow big hearts to survive what they have been through, but that they can choose to wither and die from narrowness, meanness and resentment, or embrace the wider world and live. "Plan to live in a grander world, Francis," she advises him, "not just in your skin. The world is your inheritance. Don't let a mean, limiting vision dictate what is your inherit-ance" (Persaud 1993, 94). She tells him that if she had youth and money on her side, she would wear a different dress from a different culture each day of the year. Her vision cools Francis's anger – he believes the Indian teachers discouraged his friendship with Sastra – but he regards Milly as an idealistic dreamer. Dreaming and idealism are things she shares with Rabindranath, her employer.

The novel rejects utilitarianism as a moral philosophy, but clearly embraces the universalism, individualism and egalitarianism which Jones (1999) sees as the core values of cosmopolitanism, the ethic which he believes undergirds liberal political theory. If he is right, this gives us a way of locating Milly's and Sastra's choices philosophically. At its core, the novel espouses a liberal ethic based on its cosmopolitan outlook.

After Sastra's departure for Canada, her parents reflect on the karmic predictions. Narayan remains convinced that they made no sense. Parvatee has a different view, but decides to keep her opinions to herself; she does not want to irritate a good man who always has his daughter's interest at heart, and does what he thinks is right. The reader is left to draw his or her own conclusions about the credibility of karma, as it is presented in the novel.

It is clear that some of the predictions do come to pass. Rabindranath succeeds in making Sastra "fly". Their decision to go against tradition does cause pain and sorrow, and the life and faith of the persons close to her are adversely "handicapped". But the upheavals are hardly of tsunamic pro-portions, an indication, perhaps, of the familiar tendency of soothsayers to exaggerate.

Some well-known victims of fate, such as Oedipus and the Sufi of Baghdad, learn in advance part of the destiny that awaits them. That is not the case here. Sastra's parents apparently keep the predictions to themselves. Rabindranath expresses disbelief in karma even while fulfilling it. The novel entertains belief in karma as a possibility, but seems to take the view that even such ancient beliefs have to be interpreted in the context of a wider modern world.

Sastra affirms that individuals can see their culture as antithetical to their well-being, especially when they value experiences like joy and wholeness of being above more traditional rewards. Sastra does not regret her choice, and this suggests that she is satisfied that she has acted in her own best interest. But while siding with a liberal ethic, the novel demonstrates that the freedom to choose comes at a price. Sastra's acceptance of the responsibility that comes with this freedom is perhaps the novel's strongest endorsement of this ethic.

After their wedding, Rabindranath shows Sastra the jewels which have been handed down to him from his ancestors. They are a symbol of the novel's message: "What they saw was not jewels fixed in some immutable way, but an array of energy, of flames, of lights in movement, in constant flux" (Persaud 1993, 221). This is a reflection of their lives. But it also suggests that in the modern world, belief in karma, too, may have to face the possibility of transition.

Chapter 9

The Morality of Reparations in *Salt*

According to Caribbean folklore, the eating of salt results in a loss of spiritual power. More specifically, many descendants of enslaved Africans believed that if they ate salt they would be unable to fly back to Africa. But a salt-free diet was difficult, or even impossible, in societies in which imported salted fish and pork were staples in the slaves' diet. Salt therefore came to be associated with forced exile in the Caribbean.

Anthropologists and other scholars interested in African retentions in the region have tried to explain the origin of this belief. Chevannes (1995) cites Schuler's account of the Ba Kongo identification of the Atlantic Ocean with their *kalunga*: the water which separates the living from the land of the ancestors, the return from which required a salt-free diet as the ancestors, the source of spiritual power, do not eat salt. Warner-Lewis (2003) refers to the Roman Catholic ritual of putting salt on the tongues of the baptized, a practice which it was believed by the Africans separated them from the magical knowledge – like that of flying – of their own traditions. Whatever its socio-historical origin, aspects of the belief still survive in the Caribbean. Rastafarians avoid eating salt preferring ital (vital) foods.

In Revivalism, salt intake is used to exclude the entering of spirits into mourners. In the Jamaican vernacular, to be "salt" is to be in a condition of prevailing misfortune.

Earl Lovelace's novel *Salt* (1996) is one of a small but apparently growing number of novels which deal with the issue of reparations. In this novel, the presence of salt signifies the condition of black people who have received no compensation for their exile and exploitation on the "penitential island" of Trinidad and, by extension, the Caribbean (Lovelace 1996, 44). Lovelace uses fiction to dramatize the historical experiences of those who have sought compensatory justice.

The reparation issue is of interest to many, including legal scholars, historians and moral philosophers. Legal scholars are interested in questions like the legality of slavery, the bearing of concepts like the statute of limitations on the issue, and precedents of reparation in the history of law. In the Caribbean, historians like Satchell (2000) investigate the empirical evidence that show the impact of slavery on the economies and social conditions of Caribbean countries. Philosophers like Boxill (2003) are interested in the question of the moral justifiability of reparation claims. They seek to locate the issue in traditional philosophical discourse, and to introduce moral concepts like compensatory justice, equality and human rights into the debate.

My aim here is not to defend or oppose reparations, nor to rehearse the many arguments which have been presented on either side of the question. I hope instead to elucidate the literary case which Lovelace makes for reparations, his moral reflection on the issue. Along the way I will bring some philosophical commentary to bear on my interpretations of his position.

Although he may not be the protagonist, I would like to suggest that the character Bango represents the philosophical heart of the novel. He lives on a plantation in Cascadu where his family has lived since slavery. He earns his living as a craftsman, making jewellery and curios from coconut shells and dried coconuts. He is perceived by the woman who is to become his wife as someone who "owned nothing but himself" (Lovelace 1996, 136).

Like his ancestors, he is landless. Scruton (1996) points out that psychologically, the acquisition of land symbolizes a person's permanent attachment to a particular place, his or her submission to the state's authority over the land, and an acceptance of the responsibility which accompanies such ownership. Bango, through his knowledge of stories of his ancestors, has a deep historical awareness of landlessness. Guinea John, his great-great-great-grandfather, "put two corn cobs under his armpits and flew away to Africa" (Lovelace 1996, 3). But he does not transmit this dangerous knowledge of flight and levitation to his heavy, salt-eating children. Jojo, who is Guinea John's salted grandson and Bango's grandfather, is disappointed with emancipation. After "having planted the land without reward . . . having built houses without occupying them . . . having sown without reaping" (p. 173), Bango finds his long-delayed freedom, without reparations, hollow. He rejects squatting as an option as this would only make him a second-class citizen. Instead, he chooses to continue working on the plantation while waiting for justice. In the hope of helping to bring about this justice, he presents a petition to Carabon, the owner of the estate, demanding reparation "in the interest of justice, of humanity, of harmonious relationships existing in the future between those who have profited from our captivity and those of us who have been captives" (pp. 181–82). He points out that the enslavers were compensated but the victims were not.

It is important to note that justice, humanity and social harmony are the three philosophical ideals which form the basis of his moral argument. Some reflections on all three might be helpful.

The principle of justice lies at the heart of moral philosophy and related disciplines like political philosophy and the philosophy of economics. Jojo sees injustice in the unequal compensation which emancipated slaves have received, compared to their former masters. He also remarks on the unfair division of the profits from slavery. This topic has been hotly debated since Eric Williams's well-known argument that these profits contributed to the success of the industrial revolution, to those who argue that, far from being a "miracle", the dominance of the West in the modern world has its basis in slavery and colonialism (Mills 1997a). So central is the concept of justice to the reparations debate that Boxill (2003, 134) argues that its negation ought to be invoked by redefining "reparation" as "repairing losses and deficiencies that result from injustice".

Jojo appeals to an ideal vision of humanity that dates from the 1830s, when the French Revolution, then less than fifty years old, made the ideas of liberty, equality and fraternity part of the foundations of the Enlightenment project. These concepts also helped to inspire the Haitian Revolution.

Today, these ideals are commonplace, even if not always acted upon. Fraternity, or the brotherhood of man, is defended not only in ethics and religion but in genetics. But this was not always so, certainly not in the days of slavery. Singer (1981) argues that the history of morality is an "expanding circle". As reason and the concept of impartiality became more important in modern ethics, "[t]he circle of altruism has broadened from the family and tribe to the nation and race, and we are beginning to recognize that our obligations extend to all human beings" (Singer 1981, 120). If Singer's interesting thesis is correct, it raises questions about the legitimacy of moral judgements which members of the outer parts of the circle pass on those closer to the centre. Perhaps one's historical juncture is always an important factor in moral judgements, but this raises questions about ethical relativism versus ethical objectivism which cannot be considered here. It is, however, worth noting that Jojo articulates a very modern form of humanism, one that we encounter before the middle of the nineteenth century.

Jojo's argument that ethnic relations will improve with reparations is an appeal to the consequentialist ethics of Utilitarianism. If Hare (1986) is correct, he could also have used a consequentialist argument to show why slavery was wrong. (And remains so – if reports of widespread slavery in contemporary Africa are true.) It is worth noting that some opponents of reparations argue that they would damage ethnic relations.

Jojo has learnt to "conjure power out of his situation of powerlessness" (Lovelace 1996, 171). In time, he comes to accept that he does not even know the part of Africa that is his ancestral home. His life as a wandering musician and womanizer leads him to the conclusion that the best thing he can do with the land where he has laboured in vain is to turn it into a "battleground for freedom" (p. 173), in order to make a home for himself in his new world.

Bango, his descendant, is a proud man who continues this tradition of struggle. As captain of the cricket team and leader of the steelband, he is something of a community leader. He is also reputed to be waiting for a grant of land from the government.

Bango earns his living as a craftsman, but he is by vocation something of an artist. At least he has an artist's understanding of the importance of symbolism, especially when it takes the form of ritual and ceremony. For many years he has, at his own expense, equipped a band of boys who represent the country's multiethnic population, helping them to participate in the Independence Day parade. Independence Day is as disappointing to him as Emancipation Day had been for Jojo – the novel stresses the similarities between them. Neither brings reparation. But Bango persists with his marches, hoping to convey through them the society's collective responsibility for reparations to Afro-Trinidadians. His marching has some of the characteristics of personal ritual, but it is a ritual which he hopes will come to have the wider social meaning of a national ceremony. Bango may not expect these marches to have the magical effects which some cultures traditionally associate with rituals, but he certainly intends them to have an impact, if only as a form of communication. Eventually the marches become so well known that a number of people come to believe that Bango deserves some form of national recognition for them.

The crucial turning point in the novel occurs when Bango meets Alford George, the teacher-turned-politician who believes that giving land to Bango is the right thing to do. Sitting in the prime minister's chair – symbolically and perhaps prophetically – Alford, the protagonist of the novel, listens as Bango states his case:

> I ain't come here to make the whiteman the devil. I not here to make him into another creature inhabiting another world outside the human order. I grant him no licence to pursue wickedness and brutality. I come to call him to account, as a brother, to ask him to take responsibility for his humanness, just as I have to take responsibility for mine. And if you think it is easy for either one of us, then you make an error. (pp. 167–68)

Bango does not set out to demonize the white man. He thinks evil is the result of the stupidity which he regards as the dominant characteristic of human nature. Like Jojo, he appeals to the white man's humanity, which presumably includes an acknowledgement of his capacity for stupidity and evil, as well as for the positive morality to which he is appealing. Bango appeals to the white man as a brother, as an equal, and spells out the brotherhood-of-man ideal which is more implicit in the case that Jojo makes. Bango also adds the concept of responsibility to his moral argument. To borrow some terminology from Duff (2000), Bango could have said that the white man has retrospective moral responsibility for what he has done, as well as prospective responsibility for Jojo's anticipated ethnic harmony, and all the other goods which defenders of reparation believe could flow from it. Of course, there are well-known difficulties in identifying the actual persons (in Europe, Africa and the Americas) who were responsible for slavery, as well as those persons now living who are to be held responsible for paying reparations (Vanterpool 2003). Furthermore, one is morally responsible only for what is in one's power to do. Mills (1997a) refers to an estimate that it would require more than the total wealth of the United States to pay reparations to the descendants of slaves in that country.

When Bango is offered land by Alford he tells Miss Myrtle. "If they give me the land they must do it openly. In front of everybody. People must know why they giving land to me. It must be public" (Lovelace 1996, 164). Miss Myrtle, his wife, is puzzled; she thinks he should be happy to finally receive land. She discovers that instead of trying to buy the land on which they have been living, his struggle all along has been to "make the land witness to his undefeat" (p. 155). She comes to understand Bango's belief that given his history, and that of all Afro-Trinidadians, if the demands of justice, humanity, ethnic harmony and responsibility are to be met, some form of public, socially therapeutic symbolism is required.

One of the interesting things about this novel's perspective on the reparations issue is that its arguments and literary rhetoric are directed not only at the former colonizers but at the elected government of Trinidad and Tobago. The novel suggests that the government has failed to use its power in accordance with moral principles, to secure the reparations due to all Afro-Trinidadians. Of course, this is understandable since most Caribbean nations – unlike those with African populations in the Americas – are self-governed predominantly by black people. In the novel, this political power is represented by Alford George, whose perspective we will now consider.

The teacher-turned-politician is a well-known social phenomenon in West Indian life. Since they were among the earliest to receive the benefits of Western education in the post-emancipation period, teachers were often expected to provide political leadership as well. Unsurprisingly, the teacher-politician has become a motif in West Indian fiction; it recurs elsewhere in Lovelace's work, for example in *The Wine of Astonishment*.

The link between political and educational thought is at least as old as Plato. Like Lamming's *Castle* and Brodber's *Myal*, *Salt* offers a critique of colonial educational policy and points to a new way forward. The novel suggests that the state has failed to use its teaching power, to borrow a phrase from Tussman (1977), to educate children about how to live in their own country. At the end of the novel Alford has exhausted his political career but finds himself ready to start a new one in education, one which offers the hope that he may yet contribute to a greater sense of moral responsibility in the exercise of state power.

Structurally, the novel is mostly an account of Alford's long journey to his illuminating encounter with Bango. He goes from being a dumb child to being a spokesman for reparations. Part of his journey is summarized as follows:

> Some people are born great, some achieve greatness, some have greatness thrust upon them. Alford George was guided to greatness: his childhood dumbness, his efforts to leave the island, the Exhibition class, his mental breakdown, the method of his entry into the National Party, the circumstances that gave rise to his nomination mapped a trace of events that couldn't have *just happened* and he was convinced that he had a great work ahead of him. (Lovelace 1996, 122)

Like Bango, he is a child of landless parents living on the Carabon estate in Cascadu. His father has a dream of one day buying the land, and he is buying bricks to build a home of his own. But, as a young man, Alford does not see the island as his home. He begins acquiring the educational and social skills that he believes will prepare him for the real world, outside of Trinidad. He becomes a trained teacher and is asked to teach the College Exhibition class, but when he discovers that his task is to help a small number of students escape from the island, he suffers a mental breakdown. He embarks on a mission to change the education system so that it will teach children how to live in their own country. His mission takes the dramatic form of public fasting. He becomes a public figure and his supporters urge him to form a political party. Instead he decides to become a member of the governing National Party, hoping to change politics from within. But he gets caught up in the headiness of power and, distracted by the trappings of office, he forgets his original mission. Even so he does manage to formulate a political philosophy: "Seeing Ourselves Afresh" (p. 122). Followed by newspaper reporters, he tours the island articulating his mission of indigenization, and of creating a new place in the world. But the public regards him as a pappyshow. In time, he comes to regard himself as just another overseer on the plantation.

During his voluminous reading, Alford discovers that the colonial government's post-emancipation land policy was designed to produce people like Bango. In one of his post-coital musings with his girlfriend,

Florence, Alford tells her what he has deduced from the *Royal Gazette*: "Bango is a victim of this deliberate plan set down from the beginning to prevent people working their way out of enslavement" (p. 106).

He concludes that Bango, and people like him, were deliberately wronged by the colonial government and therefore deserve compensation. He decides to work along with Adolphe Carabon, the descendant of the plantation-owning family currently in charge of the estate, and Sonan Lochan, an emerging politician of Indian descent, to present Bango with the land. Ethelbert B. Tannis, one of the island's influential political figures, reports that it is Alford's intention to make the presentation of this land "an example from his district for the whole nation" (p. 194). To give the presentation the required symbolism and power, it will be done during the Independence Day ceremony which would incorporate Bango's march. As the representative of the ethnic group which believes that, because of its longer history there and its years of forced labour, it has the greatest claim to the country, Bango would also use the occasion to officially welcome the other ethnic groups to the island. But, as we shall see, Alford's plan is frustrated.

Approximately one-third of the population of Trinidad and Tobago is of African descent, another third is of Indian descent, the remainder is ethnically diverse. In the novel, Miss Myrtle's sister points to the lack of unity among the various ethnic groups in Cascadu: the Africans, Europeans, Indians and Chinese are all going their separate ways. Ethelbert B. Tannis observes that the only thing that unites them is their sense of victimhood.

A multiethnic ethos seems appropriate in such a society. Meek (2000–2001) observes that the novel leans towards the position that Trinidadian identity is to be equated with Afro-Trinidadian identity. Adolphe Carabon and Sonan Lochan appear as major characters near the end of the novel, too late, she seems to think, for the novel to take the multiethnic ethic seriously. This seems a fair comment. But it is worth noting that cross-ethnic literary portrayals are probably more common in the Caribbean and Latin America than in most other places, and that this is a sign of promise.

Near the end of the novel, the Carabon family assembles for their father's birthday party. The old man has long wrestled with the issue of reparations, and had reserved a piece of land for this purpose, while working on an apology. He was surprised that the prime minister had not requested it, in spite of being reputed to be "the third most intelligent man in the world" (Lovelace 1996, 212). Adolphe has some of his father's good-will towards the "Blackpeople", and tries to relate to and to identify with them. His siblings distrust these inclinations and believe they disqualify him from being a leader of their race. But the Carabons also have an iden-tity issue: they feel like aliens in the country, even though they have been there before the Africans and the Indians.

The purpose of their assembly is also to discuss the reparations issue. Michael, the lawyer, refuses to feel any guilt over slavery and coloniza-tion. St Hilaire, the priest, believes that reparations are not their fami-ly's responsibility, but that of the whole society. Then it is revealed that Adolphe intends to march with Alford and Lochan on Independence Day, in support of reparations to Bango.

Lochan is the strongest representative of the Indian presence in the novel. He is the grandson of an enterprising and successful businessman who fails to win political office. The grandfather represents the long failure of Indians to be dominant in Trinidadian politics. Africans have domi-nated, perhaps as a reaction against the powerlessness they experienced under slavery. But this situation has been changing, and Lochan represents the emergence of Indian political power.

The novel portrays Indian indentureship as one of the factors con-tributing to the repression of Afro-Trinidadians. Indian characters on contract, with paper giving them access to land, prevail over both Jojo and Bango, but the novel suggests that the resulting Indocentricity con-strains them. As a young cricketer, Lochan's batting is paralysed by his always having to bat for his race. Now, with his political career taking off, he realizes that he can overcome this paralysis by batting for a larger cause. The first step towards this wider mission is to participate in the presentation of land to Bango, and to take part in the symbolism of the Independence Day parade.

The prime minister refuses to go along with Alford's proposal to present land to Bango. His party's publicly stated reason is that it would stir up racial discord. They disagree with Jojo's view that it would enhance ethnic harmony. When Alford refuses to back down, he is fired from the Cabinet. He opts to resign from politics. He contemplates writing newspaper articles and perhaps starting an independent school. He has a new mission and an unfinished house that he is building in Cascadu.

The novel's thesis is also reflected in the relationships that develop between its leading male and female characters. Vera, a young woman from Cascadu who is studying business, has a brief relationship with Alford. She leaves him after he decides not to migrate and thereby open an exit for her as well. She reappears in his life as a cleaning woman in the office building where he works, at the height of his political power. She looks at him with eyes that ask the question: "*What is he doing here?*" (p. 127).

Gloria Ollivera is his colleague at the local school. She migrates to England, with his encouragement, because he refuses to ask her to marry him and remain in the island. He believes he has to stay in the country and save the children from harms that he does not yet fully understand. Both of these women are connected with Alford's growing nationalism and individualism.

Florence is the major woman in Alford's life. She discovers her blackness through playing carnival as a Nubian princess. She believes in Mother Mabel's prophecy that the man destined for her will see her sitting on her sister's verandah in Cunaripo. Out of the many men she sees passing, she picks Alford as the one and pursues him. She becomes a part of his political organization as well as his lover, advisor and guardian. Her main function in the novel is to help Alford find himself, especially with respect to Bango and the perceived moral, social and political rightness of reparation. Meek (2000–2001) suggests that the novel's position is that the well-being of Afro-Trinidadians is a necessary condition for the creation of a peaceful multiethnic society in Trinidad. Having helped Alford discover himself and his true mission, she believes her mission has been accomplished and she decides to leave him.

Alford's failure to find a permanent mate is probably symbolic of his unfinished political task. At the end of the novel, he and Florence do not walk down the aisle or drive into the sunset, Hollywood Style. It ends with Alford's failure and with his discovery of a new beginning.

Miss Myrtle is Bango's wife. As a young mother with a child (Vera), she goes to live with Bango against the advice of her sister Shirley who is suspicious of his good looks, and his seemingly unjustified pride. Miss Myrtle supports his self-financed marches for nearly twenty years, but gets to the point where she thinks he should discontinue them. She goes to Alford to ask him to try and persuade Bango to stop. The result is that she comes to understand the significance of his marches. She also comes to appreciate that she has been his partner in an important struggle. She wants to continue to help him live his life in order to make a point.

The novel seems to say that Bango, the rebel with a morally justifiable cause, deserves a woman. Alford, a failed educator and politician who has just discovered a purpose for his life, is not yet ready.

Salt addresses the question of how state power should be used – one of the central questions of political philosophy. It is a fictional dramatization of how a postcolonial state can fail to use its power to act in accordance with the moral ideals of justice, humanity, responsibility and the rational self-interest of its society. This is dramatized by the state's unwillingness to secure reparations for those of its citizens who have been disadvantaged by history. Near the end of the novel, Bango's nephew – one of the voices in this multivocal narrative, to borrow Rahim's (1999) description of it – asks: "What is power if power is too weak to take responsibility to uphold what it is to be human?" (Lovelace 1996, 257). The tragedy of his time, he says, "is to have lost the ability to feel loss, in the inability of power to rise to its responsibility" (p. 259). What has come to be called "people power", or "the power of the powerless" as it was reportedly called by Vaclav Havel (Ball

1993, 553), has been a striking feature of world politics in recent times. It is also Bango's power. No physical power comes out of the barrels of the wooden guns carried by his boys. But true artist that he is, Bango understands the power of his symbolism, including the militarism of the boys' khaki uniforms and berets.

The Independence Day ceremony proceeds without the presence of Carabon and Lochan. The novel suggests that the society is not yet ready for Alford's new-found communalism and collective responsibility. As he joins the march, Bango's young nephew concludes that the march is "for all our own lives and had to be carried on, even if it took us to the very end of time" (Lovelace 1996, 260). The march seems necessary for the journey out of saltness.

It is sometimes said that the criticism of life is one of the functions of literature. Apparently inspired by real events, people and institutions in the history of Trinidad and Tobago, this novel offers such a criticism. Regarding Bango's optimism and the novel's hopes concerning the possible achievements of reparation, we are left to ponder a saying by the Tiv people of West Africa: "Once a great wrong has been done, it never dies. People speak the words of peace, but their hearts do not forgive. Generations perform ceremonies of reconciliation but there is no end" (Marshall 1969, epigraph).

Chapter 10

Plato versus Kincaid?
A Reading of *The Autobiography of My Mother*

Plato is both a great philosopher and an outstanding literary artist, and these two aspects of his genius meet, perhaps most famously, in his Allegory of the Cave. In this parable, ordinary humans are described as prisoners in a cave, able to see only the shadows of figures who stand outside the entrance to the cave, illuminated by the light of a fire. In such circumstances, says Plato, the prisoners come to regard the shadows as reality. If one of them were made to stand up, turn around and face the light, he would experience discomfort and vexation, and would have great difficulty adjusting his vision to the real world. Indeed, he would conclude that the real world is illusory. But he could gradually be made to adjust his vision and to look at the sun, to discover that it is the source of all that is seen in the world. In his new state of illumination he would feel sorry for his companions in the cave, and should he return there he would experience difficulty in readjusting his eyes to the darkness. His companions would laugh at his story of enlightenment, and tell him that his experience had ruined his vision. If he tried to lead them towards the light, they would probably kill him. The allegory is a metaphor of Plato's philosophy of human emancipation.

Feminist philosophers have long criticized what they see as the masculinism of Western philosophy, and Plato is one of their main targets. Kotzin (2000, 15–16), for example, accuses him of "attitudinal misogyny". She acknowledges that he boldly advocated sexual equality in the selection of the philosopher-rulers of his ideal *polis* (from as early as around the fourth century BCE), but she sees "a disdain for women" in many of his writings. By modern and contemporary standards, she contends, he is no feminist.

My focus here will be on a critique of Plato's Allegory of the Cave advanced by Luce Irigaray (1985), the French philosopher, psychoanalyst and linguist. Chanter (2000, 405) suggests that Irigaray is more accurately described as a "theorist of sexual difference" than as a feminist philosopher. The heart of feminism is widely perceived as the advocacy of sexual equality in the social, economic and political realms. This, she argues, is not Irigaray's mission. Her main concern, Chanter believes, is to articulate female subjectivity and to explore what it means to be a woman, without always defining women in terms of their relations with men.

In her book *Speculum of the Other Woman*, Irigaray (1985) offers a psychoanalytic interpretation of Plato's allegory in which she uses mimicry to subvert his views. I wish to argue that in her novel, *The Autobiography of my Mother*, Jamaica Kincaid (1996) uses characterization and narrative to achieve similar results. Irigaray's interpretations are interesting and suggestive, and much of what is said here will rest on their plausibility. But I shall try to show that these two writers, one a philosopher and the other a novelist, are united in a mission to explore female subjectivity.

I shall take from Irigaray my interpretations of what seems to be some of her main claims:

> 1. That the allegory suppresses the mother. This is based on her view that the cave is a metaphor for Mother Earth. For Plato, however, it is a place of chains, imprisonment and illusion. Knowledge of the true and the good, for him, is to be found outside the cave. The cave is a place of darkness and ignorance to which the enlightened do not want to return.

2. The allegory has a negative attitude to the womb. This is based on her comparison of their anatomical similarities. The speculum of her title is a medical instrument used to examine the body's cavities, and she compares its imagery with Plato's methods. The prisoner is taken by force from the cave/womb through a passage that resembles a vagina and a stealthily removed hymen.

3. Both (1) and (2) combine to indicate an unwillingness to acknowledge men's dependence on women. Irigaray thinks Plato's allegory suppresses this fact.

4. By its refusal to acknowledge the importance of the feminine, this historically early and famous allegory has played a significant role in the development of an anti-feminist ideology in the West. This ideology sees the feminine as something constructed by men, and denies that women can and should be the producers of their own discourse. For Irigaray, therefore, the allegory is part of the philosophical and historical backdrop against which women should affirm their difference. (Irigaray 1985; Grimshaw and Fricker 1996; Chanter 1999, 2000)

I shall examine Kincaid's novel in the light of these views.

Most readers of Kincaid's novels will recognize that the loss of a mother is a recurring theme, some would say the dominant theme – in her work. As Simmons (1994) observes, the betrayal of the biological mother is paralleled by that of the British colonial "mother" country. The yearning for a dead mother is the central theme of *Autobiography*. So if we accept Irigaray's interpretation of Plato's allegory, we could say that on the topic of recognizing the importance of the mother, Plato and Kincaid go in opposite directions.

The novel is the autobiography of Xuela Claudette Richardson, a Dominican woman of Carib, African and Scottish descent. Her Carib mother dies at the moment she is born, and this fact shapes the rest of her life. The Caribbean derives its name from the Caribs, one of the region's indigenous peoples who were defeated and almost annihilated by the European colonizers. Xuela's yearning after her dead mother is therefore symbolic of the region's search for an identity to be found in its origins. It is part of Xuela's tragedy – and perhaps the Caribbean's as well – that this mother was someone who was unable to protect herself and her child from the world's cruelty.

Xuela's yearning for her mother ranges from the metaphysical to the epistemological and the psycho-social. I shall examine each in turn.

Xuela sees her mother as a presence standing between herself and eternity. When her mother dies, this link is broken, leaving "a bleak, black wind" at Xuela's back (Kincaid 1996, 3). Eternity is a philosophically interesting concept in which some mode of existence is conceptualized as having no beginning and no end. For Plato, eternity is in the realm of Being, in the Forms beyond the phenomenal world of appearance and becoming. But Xuela seems to locate eternity in history and the continuity of generations. It is this gap in the continuity of history that puts a bleak wind behind her back. Her yearning for a link with eternity through her mother is not for something like Platonic transcendence, but, as we shall see, for the psycho-social experiences of the phenomenal, or cave-like world, as Irigaray would say. She hopes to connect with eternity inside the cave, not outside it. So, metaphysically, she is also opposed to Plato.

Attaining knowledge of her mother is Xuela's major epistemological quest. She describes her mother as "the very big thing" that she does not know (p. 28). The big knowledge for Plato is that of the Forms, especially that of The Good, and it is to be found by getting out of the cave. The big knowledge for Xuela is that of the cave/mother.

In the absence of direct knowledge of her mother – we could call it Russell's knowledge by acquaintance – Xuela resorts to hearsay and imagination as her main modes of cognition in the search for her mother. Hearsay informs her that her mother was also a motherless child, and that she was abandoned in front of a nunnery when she was a baby. Xuela imagines her being raised by the nuns to be a "quiet, shy, long-suffering, unquestioning, modest, wishing-to-die-soon person" (p. 199). The relationship between her mother and her father is also something which she constructs in her imagination. Unable to imagine her father responding to her mother's beauty – if she had any – or taking an interest in the fate of the Carib people, she nevertheless imagines him being drawn to her "sadness, her weakness, her long-lost-ness, the crumbling of ancestral lines, her dejectedness, the false humility that was really defeat" (p. 200). She thinks of her father as someone who would find beauty in such qualities. If he was saddened by her mother's death, as rumoured, Xuela does not believe that it made him a more compassionate person.

In her psycho-social yearnings we find Xuela longing to see her mother's face, seeing her in recurring dreams, and having reflections on her evoked by certain natural and social settings. The art of portraiture in painting, sculpture and photography reflects the psychological importance of the human face to all of us. Not surprisingly, Xuela longs to see her mother's face: "I missed the face I had never seen"; and "I could not see spirits at all, I was just looking for that face, the face I would never see, even if I lived forever" (p. 5). But she never sees her mother's face, not even in her dreams.

She has a recurring dream in which she sees her mother descending – never ascending – a ladder. But she sees only the hem of her white gown and her heels. In one of the dreams, her mother sings a song without words, not a lullaby, nor a sentimental song intended to calm her. Nevertheless, Xuela treasures the sound of her mother's voice as a source of contentment and pleasure.

Thoughts about her mother are evoked in certain natural settings. The dreams begin while she is sleeping at a spot covered with stones. She also thinks about her mother at a time of day that she associates with loss.

Certain social situations also evoke dreams and thoughts of her mother. One of Xuela's most powerful dreams occurs during the first night she spends in her father's house after meeting his new wife, who hates her. She can tell from the way people look at her that they see the Carib in her more than they see the African, and this makes her think of her mother. Xuela is not afraid of being the only girl in her class because her mother is already dead – she believes that a dead mother is the only reason a child should have for being afraid. In the ledger of life which she begins to con-struct in her mind while living with the La Battes in Roseau, the loss of her mother precedes the loss of youth and love. When her father tries to claim ownership of her, she resists, she would have consented to be owned by her mother, but since this did not happen she refuses to be owned by anyone. The observed reality of her father's death lends a contrasting illusory quality to the more distant death of her mother. But the realization that she is now an orphan makes her feel that this experience is the beginning of adulthood.

The social object which evokes Xuela's most powerful reflections on her mother is her mother's lamp. Xuela keeps it in her room at the house where she works as a doctor's servant. Its light brings two strong associations to her mind. First, that it shone on both her mother's death as well as on her own birth. Second, that her mother saw her father's face by its light, right after he had impregnated her with Xuela.

There are two aspects to the symbolism of light in Plato's allegory. The fire in the cave casts the shadows of illusion. But the sun is the symbol of the transcendent realm of knowledge of the true and the good. For Xuela, the lamplight shines only on the human phenomena of conception, birth and death. And these are fundamental realities for the cave mother.

Unlike Plato, in Irigaray's interpretation, Xuela is strongly pro-mother. But like Plato, she (and presumably the author) seems surprisingly anti-womb for most of the novel. None of the major female characters is successful in their reproductive function. There are many references to wombs and inner spaces, and they are mostly characterized negatively.

While she is a teenager, Xuela's father arranges for her to live with the La Battes, a childless couple who live in Roseau, the capital of Dominica. Madame La Batte "wanted a child, but her womb was like a sieve; it would not contain a child, it would not contain anything now" (p. 70). In what is presented as child-rape, Monsieur La Batte impregnates Xuela. The impregnation has the approval of Madame La Batte who sees this as a way of getting the child she wants. But on discovering that she is pregnant, Xuela runs away and has an abortion which makes her feel like someone in a black hole. After the abortion, she experiences a feeling of emptiness: "Inside me there was nothing; inside me there was a vault made of a substance so heavy I could find nothing to compare it to" (p. 99). After the removal of the foetus, her life circumstances make her feel like someone moving from one black hole to another.

Still there is a suggestion that she does not regard inner spaces in entirely negative terms. She thinks of parts of her childhood as events that happened in a small, dark place into which she can peer from above. In this place "different things are in the shadows at different times, different things are in the light" (p. 33). There are the shadows of motherlessness, but also the light of exhilarating moments in a beautiful landscape.

Roland, the man she says she loves, is unable to understand why she will not bear his children. Once, while she is with him "Feeling my womb contract I crossed the room, still naked; small drops of blood spilled from inside me, evidence of my refusal to accept his silent offering" (p. 175). Not even love can make her reproduce.

The frequently masturbating Xuela is capable of sexual desire, which she describes as follows: "the feeling was a sweet hollow feeling, an empty space with a yearning to be filled, to be filled up until the yearning was exhausted" (p. 154). Her sexual desire is stirred by Philip, the English doctor she does not love, but whom she eventually marries. In any case having children with Philip in marriage is out of the question since "[b]y the time I had married my own womb had dried up, shrivelled, like an old piece of vegetable matter left out too long" (p. 206). For Xuela, even her marriage does not lead to reproduction.

In a sense, Xuela becomes a dying mother herself as she refuses to be a mother to children: "I would never become a mother, but that would not be the same as never bearing children. I would bear children, but I would never be a mother to them" (p. 97). She describes a fantasy in which she visits God-like tribulations and destruction on the large numbers of children she would bear.

The other major female characters do not fare much better. Like Xuela, Philip's former wife Moira also "had a broken womb" although Xuela does not know if it was from birth or, as in her case, done deliberately (p. 157).

The new wife of Xuela's father, who is characterized in the tradition of the evil stepmother, does overcome her initial barrenness to bear a son and a daughter. The son dies in childhood from a terrible disease. The daughter is disabled by a bicycle accident, and the child which her husband fathers with another woman dies.

The novel contains no accounts of wanted children successfully conceived, born and raised. Instead, it chronicles stories of sieve-like, and shrivelled wombs, and of children who are born but fail to thrive and reproduce. At first glance it seems to be a novel about failing wombs, about wombs failing to do what wombs in the normal course of nature are supposed to do. I call this attitude to the womb Platonic, in the Irigarayan sense.

But when we get to the end of the novel, we discover that the autobiography is an imagined life of her mother, as well as the account of her own life which would have been given by the children she did not have. She says, "This is an account of the person who was never allowed to be and an account of the person I did not allow myself to become" (p. 228).

Kincaid is engaged in the kind of hypothetical thinking philosophers call thought experiments (Gooding 2000). She makes Xuela imagine the possible autobiography of a woman in certain Caribbean circumstances. It is a character and story many will find unattractive as it includes, among other things, abortion, adultery, childlessness, "sexual devouring" (Morris 2002, 954), sadomasochism (Holcomb and Holcomb 2002), and failure of sustained reproduction. It is not a life lived, but another life, one which is presumably intended to be morally deplorable, but which can nevertheless be imagined as a consequence of certain historical and social circumstances.

In terms of the novel's poetics, the anti-womb hypothesis is presented in a way that will make us want to reject it. So on this topic, too, Kincaid is also opposed to Irigaray's Plato. It should be noted that the hypothetical thinking does not affect the novel's pro-mother stance; having a mother and yearning for one are both morally desirable.

It seems as if one of the aims of the novel is to make us imagine another, undescribed life in which women (and societies) know their mothers, have loving relationships with their fathers, marry persons they love (we will come to those two shortly) and bear thriving children.

Consciousness of men's dependence on women, a form of awareness so important to Irigaray, is not a characteristic of any of the major male characters in the novel. They all seem to be unaware of the female principle – what is called the *Yin* in Chinese philosophy. Not surprisingly, the one who comes closest to it is the one whom Xuela loves. I shall look briefly at all three: Alfred her father; Philip who becomes her husband; and Roland the man she loves but does not marry.

She describes her father as a hyphenated man, an Afro-Scot with red hair who identifies with the grapefruit which, like him, is said to have originated in the West Indies. Named after Alfred the Great, he is a policeman and jailer whose presence usually means misfortune to others. His uniform has become like a second skin to him, and the persona he presents to others is a mask so carefully constructed that it conceals a self he does not know. Xuela compares the colour of his skin to corruption, and describes him as a man who gets rich by exploiting others, including his second wife, and her connections. He is capable of loving only money, not people. He is cruel to children and people weaker than himself. His terrible suffering before he dies almost makes Xuela believe in justice. It is only after his death that something like love for him begins to stir in her.

He never speaks of his mother affectionately and does not even have a photograph of her. He seems unclear even about her physical features. Xuela finds it hard to imagine him as boy in need of a mother's nurturing. It is Xuela who imagines that his mother "must have mended his clothes, cooked his food, tended his schoolboy wounds, encouraged his ambitions, soothed his wounded brow" (Kincaid 1996, 183). She is unable to do these things, and wishes her own mother had done them for her.

Alfred does many fatherly things for her. He arranges a caregiver for her after her mother dies; he takes her to live in his home when he remarries; he gives her an education; and he gets her a job as a doctor's servant. Yet Xuela says: "I could list for him the number of times he had failed to be a father to me, his motherless child, while on his way to becoming a man of this world" (p. 113). The missing element is not spelled out but it seems that Xuela wants a father who will also mother her. But Alfred, a man so out of touch with his feminine side, his *Yin*, cannot do this.

Xuela begins as a servant to Philip, her father's friend, and ends up as his wife. According to her, he "belonged to that restless people unable to leave the world alone" (p. 209). She has no love or compassion for him. Indeed, seeing humanity in him angers her for it implies the humanity of his kind, and this raises problems for people like her and their historical experience in the Caribbean. Her sister sees their marriage as her conquest of the conqueror. But she marries him, she says, in order to transform her life into a romance; to her "Romance is the refuge of the defeated" (p. 216).

His alienation from the feminine principle – two barren wives and unfulfilled love with both – is also symbolically expressed in his hobby. He is an amateur naturalist who delights in distorting the natural behaviour of plants and animals. He is a man who is out of touch with Mother Nature.

Philip is also alienated from his motherland. He also has little affection for his wife Moira who eventually achieves a macabre unification with the Caribbean island when, after she poisons herself, with Xuela's help, she turns black in death, and assumes the colour of the people she despises. Philip loves Xuela, but it is unrequited love, so he makes no meaningful connection with the Caribbean. He remains suspended between his motherland and his exile in the Caribbean.

Roland is another married man with whom Xuela gets involved. He is a stevedore with large, thick hands. She is attracted to him at first sight. The first thing she notices is his mouth which is "like an island in the sea" (p. 163). He is gap-toothed, which is believed to be a sign of untrustworthiness, but this does not deter her. Feeling attracted, she calls out her own name to get his attention: "and when our eyes met and we laughed at the same time, I said, I love you, and he said, I know".

He smells of the cargo which he unloads from ships, and he steals cloth on the job which he gives to Xuela and his wife to make clothes. Xuela is drawn to the fact that he has a sense of himself as someone precious. Furthermore, his personal history does not contain killings, conquests and stolen birthrights. But this history contains a long list of the names of women he has loved, and this fact is important for Xuela for she says she cannot love a man who has not loved other women. Even if he does not have a consciousness of it, this history is evidence that he at least loves the female principle, and is happy to absorb its love as well. He brings an unprecedented happiness into her life. Her love for him is so intense that she wears the colour red to signify her passion. Eventually, however, she is physically attacked by Roland's wife. Afterwards Xuela says, "I would not have married a man I loved at all" (p. 205). Furthermore, she comes to see that his mouth, like the island which it resembles, contains dangerous secrets. So she abandons him.

In sum, I submit that Kincaid's pro-mother and pro-womb stance, combined with her negative portrayal of men who are out of touch with or do not acknowledge the female principle put her in opposition to Irigaray's interpretation of Plato's Allegory of the Cave. In his famous painting *The School of Athens*, Raphael portrays Plato pointing at the sky, away from the cave, while Aristotle, his former pupil, points at the earth. I believe that Kincaid has more in common with Aristotle than with Plato. She is also in the now growing tradition of the exploration and voicing of female subjectivity.

This meeting of an ancient Greek philosopher, a contemporary Belgian-French philosopher of feminine difference, and a West Indian novelist, is testimony to the universality of philosophy and its enduring link with literature.

Conclusion

All of these novels reward philosophical attention. Each deals with at least one major philosophical issue, some with more than one. Together they show some of the philosophical ideas and concerns which have been at work within West Indian literary culture. I believe this study shows that the Caribbean has serious contributions to make to philosophy and literature.

In the following summary of each novel's main issues, I have included some commentary and a few more general conclusions.

George Lamming's *In the Castle of My Skin* is a powerful dramatization of one of the central questions in the philosophy of education: What are the aims of education? By embodying the aims of colonial education in Barbados, and offering a critique of them, it raises deep questions about the aims of postcolonial education in the Caribbean.

I think that formulating the aims of education is one of the region's most important philosophical tasks, one that should be of concern to its emerging philosophers, educators, makers of educational policy and social planners. The colonial disfigurement of the history of the West Indian people and the lack of Afro-Caribbean ethnic consciousness are among Lamming's concerns. To these must be added the educational implications of globalization, rapid technological advances, environmental degradation, poverty, and increasing crime and violence, among others.

Many believe that the question of the meaning of life is the most important philosophical question of all. Roger Mais's *Black Lightning* links the ethics of suicide and the psychological evil of alienation to the difficulties of a life without meaning. These ideas are presented through the story of a Jamaican artist whose suicide is caused by his alienation from society.

The history of mass migration from the West Indies, and the estrangement it has created, especially in the young, suggest that a sense of alienation from the region is widespread. Whether or not this is linked to the suicide rate is a matter for social psychologists and sociologists. What is significant for our purposes is that Mais links these evils to the question of the role of the artist in Jamaican society. Every ethnic group in the West Indies is descended from societies in which rich artistic traditions were an integral part of life. Dislocation, slavery and indenture, in what Lewis (1983) calls mercantilist-capitalist anti-intellectual societies, caused a traumatic rupturing of these traditions, and arts and philosophy did not flourish in the new setting. This began to change when the rise of nationalism and independence movements brought about a quest for a recovery of the arts in the Caribbean. As Stuart Hall (2001, 34) reminds us, West Indians cannot "go back through the eye of the needle" to their ancestral cultures. Nevertheless, those functions of the arts which are rooted in man's biological nature will endure everywhere. West Indian artists face the challenge of combining these with whatever ancestral continuities still exist – to create the art which their new experience demands. Mais's sculptor fails to do so, but future West Indian artists are not bound to repeat his failure. It is well known that most West Indian writers live (or have lived) overseas. This includes most of the authors examined in this book. Given their dependence on the visual environment, visual artists tend to remain at home. It is probably significant, therefore, that Mais's artist is one of them, and as a sculptor, he is arguably the most elemental of artists. For these reasons, I think, a failed sculptor should give us special cause for concern.

Since it is the study of the nature of reality, many regard metaphysics as the most fundamental area of philosophy, and few aspects of human reality are more basic than the nature of the self. In my interpretation, the self is the subject of Wilson Harris's *Palace of the Peacock*. I believe that the novel describes a journey to a recognition of the self as a form of radiance.

Since it addresses fundamental issues of human nature, metaphysics undergirds the social, historical and geographical concerns which preoccupy most people. Harris's novel will interest anyone who is drawn to the metaphysical and spiritual dimensions of Caribbean thought, and anyone interested in the differences between inner and outer reality. His optimistic estimate of the self will no doubt be a consolation to those who come to share it.

I use V.S. Naipaul's A *House for Mr. Biswas* to illustrate: the question of whether or not literature can be a source of knowledge and understanding. I try to show that this novel is a source of both conceptual and empathetic knowledge, and of understanding conceived as the apprehension of disclosures about human nature, as well as a way of making sense of experience. Naipaul's protagonist overcomes the subordination imposed on him by history, and he goes on to exercise his potency by acquiring his own home and achieving a sense of order in his life. Naipaul has given the region what is arguably its most powerful symbol yet of the Caribbean as the home of an independent people. This novel can be an inspiration to virtually all disciplines pursued in the region since it goes to the heart of Caribbean aspirations.

Albert Camus, the existentialist novelist-philosopher who influenced Orlando Patterson's *The Children of Sisyphus*, regards freedom and responsibility as the main aim of life. Patterson's novel, however, is an account of the social and psychological ravages of unfreedom in a Kingston slum. Some of the characters are fatalistic and nihilistic. The novel therefore seems to be an example of existentialist nihilism.

I argue, however, that while the novel does not embody the existentialist optimism in Camus or Sartre, its critique of unfreedom can be seen as pre-existentialist, a call for the existentialist values of freedom and responsibility in Jamaican society. Its author's later interest in freedom as a moral and political ideal suggests that this was the direction of his thought. I contend that for Caribbean societies like these (which have known and still know unfreedom), there is no philosophical ideal more important than freedom.

Of all the novels examined, Jean Rhys's *Wide Sargasso Sea* is the one that deals with the widest range of philosophical issues. These are mostly moral issues, including the subjection of women, the treatment of the mentally ill (and of persons so regarded), alienation as a psychological evil, and whether some forms of violence can be justified. Against the background of the ancient view that tragedy is a literary genre of special philosophical importance, I argue that these issues are brought together to make this novel a Caribbean tragedy, and a significant feminization of the genre.

The number of issues dealt with in this small novel is truly impressive, as they also include history, ethnicity, oppression and religion. Technically and politically linked with one of the classics of English literature, it demonstrates the power of fiction to illuminate historical questions. It also raises questions about Caribbean ethnicity and the place of ethnic minorities in Caribbean literature. It deals with the religious lore of both Europeans and Africans. And it links the problem of oppression with politics, gender and ethnicity. I think this novel can also be seen as a contribution to feminist philosophy, psychology and literary theory.

Few issues are more fundamental to the philosophies of religion, education, and the social sciences, or to all thought about human destiny than the question of the concept of a person. It is a foundation stone of all these endeavours. In the Caribbean, it is likely that Western notions of this concept predominate, but it is important to note that African conceptions of a person are often quite different from those in the West, and that these too may have influenced Caribbean ways of thinking. Indeed, it is likely that a creolization of conceptions has occurred and continues to occur. I think there is a need for further philosophical and anthropological research on this question.

I argue that African-derived conceptions of a person form the basis of Erna Brodber's *Myal*. I explore the metaphysics of these African conceptions as well as their emphasis on communitarianism and (ethical) normativity, and I show how these are present in *Myal*. I stress the novel's position on authenticity as a cultural and moral value, and show how this forms the basis of its educational philosophy, both as a critique and as a positive theory.

There is a growing interest in African philosophy and in African diaspora philosophy (Mbiti 1969; Serequeberhan 1991; Appiah 1992; Hord and Lee 1995; Henry 2000; Lott and Pittman 2003; Wiredu 2004). Along with this there is also an emerging interest in the relation between African philosophy and African literature (Appiah 2004; Bidima 2004). No doubt work on the link between African philosophy and African diaspora literature will emerge in due course. My chapter on Brodber is intended as a step in this direction.

The metaphysical concept of causation is part of our everyday sense-making as well as a basic component of academic exercises like scientific and historical explanation. The law of karma is an Indian interpretation of it which is widely seen as one of the pillars of Indian philosophy. Lakshmi Persaud's *Sastra* is evidence that the concept has survived the *Kala Pani*, and has found its way into the literature of Trinidad. I examine this novel's treatment of a karmic prediction in the light of another philosophical issue raised by multiculturalism: that of the conflict which sometimes arises when persons have to choose between culture and their perceptions of their well-being. I argue that, caught between Hindu traditionalism and the attractions of Western liberalism, the novel's protagonist not only chooses the latter, but opts for a wider cosmopolitanism.

The growing body of literature by Indo-Caribbean women is a fairly recent phenomenon. It is taking place against a complex historical and cultural background which includes one of the world's oldest philosophical and literary traditions. It is hoped that the resulting novels will in time contribute much to the understanding of the Indo-Caribbean experience and the human condition in general.

The issue of reparations is an important one for all peoples who have been victims of slavery, war, oppression, and similar kinds of injustice. In *Salt*, Earl Lovelace uses historical fiction to explore the morality of this issue from the perspective of Afro-Trinidadians. The novel appeals to philosophical ideals of justice, humanism, social harmony and moral responsibility in the development of its literary argument.

This is an issue with legal, historical, political as well as moral dimensions. Lovelace employs an impressive array of literary techniques to give artistic force to his critique of the failure of the state of Trinidad and Tobago to secure reparations for its disadvantaged people, and to articulate the view that reparation is morally justified. This is thoughtful reading for those who defend as well as those who oppose reparations.

Plato's Allegory of the Cave, with its doctrine of human emancipation from bondage and darkness, is probably the most famous image in Western philosophy. But Luce Irigaray's psychoanalytic interpretation of it sees the cave as a metaphor of Mother Earth and the womb, and argues that the parable is therefore a suppression of the mother, the womb and the feminine voice. I found echoes of Irigaray's views in Jamaica Kincaid's *The Autobiography of my Mother*. I interpret her fictional autobiography of an Afro-Carib-Scot woman growing up in Dominica as pro-mother, pro-womb and critical of male characters (which would presumably include Plato) who are out of touch with the female principle. This is a novel which will encourage reflections on The Caribbean Mother, and on questions of Creole identity in the region.

In his famous painting *The School in Athens*, Raphael portrays Plato pointing to the sky while Aristotle, his former pupil, points at the earth and its people. I conclude that, if Irigaray is correct, Kincaid's philosophy is closer to Aristotle's, and so also at variance with Plato's.

I think that one of the most exciting and important developments in modern literature is the emergence of writing that describes the female sensibility. Writers like Rhys, Brodber, Persaud and Kincaid are helping to bring the Caribbean dimension of these voices to both regional and global audiences. The exploration of female subjectivity through literature, combined with philosophical reflection on our fundamental questions, could open new and exciting dimensions in the relation between philosophy and gender.

I would like to conclude with some comments on the philosophical range of our findings, the matter of ancestral philosophies and the relation between this study and Caribbean intellectual history.

The philosophical issues in these books include metaphysics (Harris, Persaud, Mais); ethics (Rhys, Lovelace); social and political philosophy (Patterson, Lovelace, Brodber, Persaud); philosophy of education (Lamming, Brodber, Lovelace); philosophy of literature (Naipaul, Rhys); aesthetics (Mais); and feminist philosophy (Rhys, Persaud, Kincaid). While social and political issues predominate, along with related concerns in ethics, education and gender, I think it is encouraging to see metaphysical questions among the concerns explored. Except for Mais, I found very little self-reflection on the role of the arts. Epistemology, which is widely regarded as second in importance only to metaphysics, is best exemplified by Naipaul's novel. I found some suggestions of philosophy of language and logic in Kincaid, but these were not explored.

Western thought is the dominant ancestral philosophical influence on these novels. The exceptions are Brodber whose work shows the influence of African thought, and Persaud whose work embodies an important component of Indian philosophy. There is probably some influence of Amerindian philosophy on some of these novels. Harris (1999) claims that the Carib bone flute has influenced all his fiction, and there is an Arawak character in his *Palace of the Peacock;* some Carib thought may also have entered Kincaid's novel through her Carib and part-Carib characters; but this possible influence is unexplored in the study. Chinese characters appear in West Indian fiction, and there is a small body of Chinese writing (Yun 2004), but I am not aware of any philosophically interesting novels by Chinese West Indians. The Chinese have a rich philosophical and literary tradition, but it seems as if this aspect of their civilization has yet to emerge in the West Indies. Similarly, I am not aware that Jewish philosophy and Islamic philosophy have had any significant impact on the West Indian novel. Jewish thought, especially that found in the Bible, has been enormously influential in the life of the region, and some of this can be found in these novels, but this influence is probably more religious than philosophical. In any case, the influence has not been scrutinized. Islam and the philosophy related to it are so influential in the contemporary world that their influence will certainly be felt in West Indian literature sooner or later. But I am not yet aware of any West Indian novels that show an Islamic influence.

I share Lamming's planetary view of the Caribbean and I take the view that West Indian novelists should not tie themselves to the influences of their own ethnicity, however understandable a temptation this might be. Ezra Pound says somewhere that what one loves well is one's true heritage. A writer is entitled to love whatever he or she finds lovable in any tradition.

Although this study is not intended as intellectual history, the fact that the novels were studied in chronological order makes it likely that its findings may have some bearing on the kind of project envisaged by Benn (2004, xix) dealing with the literary dimension of such a history. The books examined cover a mere forty-three years of development – the region has a very brief indigenous literary history – and represent a very small sample. However, I venture three observations for what they are worth. First, the women writers are all in the second half of the study. This may be a Caribbean expression of the universal women's movement. Second, there is more evidence of ethnicity and awareness of ancestral philosophies in the second half of the study. This may be an expression of an increasing awareness of ethnicity and an interest in roots. It may or may not be significant that the women writers show the greatest interest in ancestral philosophies, and that their works stir the loudest ancestral resonances. This is true in every case. Third, the study has unearthed a remarkable philosophical cosmopolitanism. To what extent this is a description of an objective reality, or a reflection of the ideological bias of the writer, is a question that invites scrutiny and reflection.

I have claimed that the questions examined in this study are universal. I have tried to show that these questions are embodied in imagined images of lived experiences in the Caribbean. But this study deals with only a few fragments of the Caribbean literary mosaic. It would be interesting if research on the literature of the Spanish-speaking, French-speaking and Dutch-speaking Caribbean reveals that philosophical as well as other linkages connect these jewels of the archipelago.

Appendix

The Authors

Erna Brodber

The scholar-artist Erna Brodber (b. 1940) is a much-honoured Jamaican novelist, sociologist, historian and community worker. She regards her fictional works as hypotheses created to guide her sociological research. Much of her work, as both scholar and artist, focuses on the Woodside community where she lives. Her work is germane to an interest in African philosophy, philosophical psychology, and the philosophy of religion.

Her other works include the novels *Jane and Louisa Will Soon Come Home* (1980), *Louisiana* (1994), and *The Rainmaker's Mistake* (2007). Her academic books include *Abandonment of Children in Jamaica* (1974), *Perceptions of Caribbean Women* (1982), *The Continent of Black Consciousness* (2003), and *Woodside, Pear Tree Grove P.O.* (2004).

Wilson Harris

Wilson Harris (b. 1921) is a Guyanese novelist, poet, essayist, critic and literary theorist. Regarded as one of the innovators of the twentieth-century novel, he rejects restrictive realism in favour of a poetic discourse which tries to capture the soul of the Caribbean as he perceives it in landscape, history and myth. Of English, Indian, African and Amerindian ancestry, he draws on all of these sources in weaving his fictions. Philosophical issues raised by his work include the nature of imagination, philosophical anthropology and the aesthetics of the novel.

His other works include the novels *The Far Journey of Oudin* (1961), *The Whole Armour* (1962), *The Secret Ladder* (1963), *The Eye of the Scarecrow* (1965), *The Tree of the Sun* (1978), *The Four Banks of the River of Space* (1990) *Jonestown* (1996), and the essays "Literacy and the Imagination", "Tradition and the West Indian Novel", and "The Unfinished Genesis of the Imagination".

Jamaica Kincaid

Jamaica Kincaid (b. 1949) is an Antiguan novelist, storywriter and writer of non-fiction. Her dominant theme is the relationship between mothers and daughters, and the suggested similarity to that between "mother" countries and their oppressed colonies. Her work is relevant to anyone interested in feminist philosophy, the philosophy of history and postcolonial philosophy of literature.

Her other works include the novels *Annie John* (1985) and *Lucy* (1990), the collection of stories *At the Bottom of the River* (1983) and the non-fiction work *A Small Place* (1988).

George Lamming

George Lamming (b. 1927) is a Barbadian novelist, poet, essayist, editor and sage. Some of the characters in his novels may be regarded as philosophers. His works also reveal an interest in existential questions, communitarianism, nationalism, and the uses and abuses of power. Widely travelled and much honoured, he is a highly respected West Indian intellectual.

His other works include the novels *The Emigrants* (1954), *Season of Adventure* (1960), *Water with Berries* (1971), *Natives of My Person* (1972), and the collection of essays *The Pleasures of Exile* (1960).

Earl Lovelace

Earl Lovelace (b. 1935) is an award-winning Trinidadian novelist, playwright, storywriter and essayist. Interested in social issues, his writings cover a range of concerns including the failures of education, civil disobedience, and the meaning of carnival. Unlike many West Indian writers, he has spent a significant part of his life writing in his home country. His work is germane to social and political philosophy, the philosophy of education, ethics and the philosophy of gender.

His other works include the novels *While Gods Are Falling* (1965), *The Schoolmaster* (1968), *The Wine of Astonishment* (1982), *The Dragon Can't Dance*, the collection of stories *A Brief Conversion and Other Stories* (1988), and the drama collection *Jestina's Calypso and Other Plays* (1984).

Roger Mais

Roger Mais (1905–1955) is a Jamaican novelist, dramatist, poet, story writer and painter. A supporter of the nationalist movement, he was imprisoned by the English colonial government for an article attacking Winston Churchill which was published in *Public Opinion*. A passionate social critic, he wrote about both the degradation and vitality of Kingston's slums, as well as the futility of life in beautiful rural landscapes. He is said to be the first West Indian writer to portray a Rastafarian protagonist in a positive light, so his work is important for the study of this philosophically significant movement, which originated in Jamaica. Mais's work also deals with the impact of colonialism, oppression and classism on contemporary Jamaica.

His other works include the novels *The Hills Were Joyful Together* (1953), *Brother Man* (1954), and the posthumously published collection of stories *Listen, the Wind (1986)*.

V.S. Naipaul

Born in Trinidad, V.S. Naipaul (b. 1932) is an internationally renowned Nobel Laureate for Literature. As novelist, travel writer and autobiographer, he has travelled the world, trying to get a clearer picture of it, as he says in his Nobel Lecture, and chronicling both the troubles of postcolonial societies, and the inadequacies of the metropolitan West. His work will be of philosophical interest to anyone interested in colonialism and morality, development ethics, and the philosophy of religion.

His other works include the novels *The Mystic Masseur* (1957), *Guerrillas* (1975), *A Bend in the River* (1979), *The Enigma of Arrival: A Novel in Five Sections* (1987), the travel writings *The Middle Passage: Impressions of Five Societies – British, French and Dutch* (1962), *Among the Believers: An Islamic Journey* (1981), *A Turn in the South* (1989), and the autobiographical texts *Finding the Centre: Two Narratives* (1984) and *Reading and Writing: A Personal Account* (2000).

Orlando Patterson

Orlando Patterson (b. 1940) is an award-winning and internationally renowned Jamaican sociologist and novelist. An example of the region's numerous scholar-artists, the imagined worlds of his novels may be seen as interpretations of the real worlds of his sociological research; in any case his work raises the interesting question of the relations between them. A major focus of his academic work seems to be the study of the dialectical relationship between two opposites: slavery and freedom. Slavery raises numerous philosophical issues, from the question of its wrongness to the call for reparations. Freedom is one of the core concepts of social and political philosophy.

His other works include the novels *An Absence of Ruins* (1967) and *Die the Long Day* (1972), and the academic texts *The Sociology of Slavery: An Analysis of the Origins, Development and Structure of Negro Slave Society in Jamaica* (1967), *Slavery and Social Death* (1982) and *Freedom*, vol. 1: *Freedom in the Making of Western Culture* (1991).

Lakshmi Persaud

Lakshmi Persaud (b. 1939) is a Trinidadian novelist, geographer and educator. She is one of the emerging voices in female Indo-Caribbean fiction, long said to be eclipsed by its Afro-Caribbean, North American and British counterparts. Her themes include the cultural continuities, and discontinuities between India and the Caribbean. Her work will interest anyone who wants to know more about Indo-Caribbean philosophy, feminist philosophy and philosophy of religion.

Her other works include *Butterfly in the Wind* (1990) and *For the Love of My Name* (2000).

Jean Rhys

Jean Rhys (1890–1979) was born in Dominica and left when she was sixteen. Most of her writing was done in England and Paris. An award winning novelist and storywriter, she achieved fame and recognition late in life. She is said to have been ahead of her time in the way she wrote about women's issues. Her themes include the exploitation of women, female sexuality and the perspective of the Creole. Her work is germane to an interest in feminist philosophy, the philosophy of history, and the question of personal identity.

Her other works include the novels *Voyage in the Dark* (1934), *After Leaving Mr Mackenzie* (1931), *Good Morning, Midnight* (1939), and the collections *The Left Bank and Other Stories* (1927) and *Tigers Are Better Looking* (1968).

References

Allison, Alexander W., et al., eds. 1970. *The Norton Anthology of Poetry*. 3rd ed. New York: Norton.

Appiah, Kwame Anthony. 1992. *In My Father's House: Africa in the Philosophy of Culture*. New York and Oxford: Oxford University Press.

———. 2004. "African Philosophy and African Literature". In *A Companion to African Philosophy*, ed. Kwasi Wiredu. Oxford: Blackwell.

Aristotle. 1961. *Poetics*. Trans. S.H. Butcher; intro. Francis Fergusson. New York: Hill and Wang.

Ayer, A.J. 1980. *Hume*. Oxford: Oxford University Press.

Ball, Terence. 1993. "Power". In *A Companion to Contemporary Political Philosophy*, ed. Robert E. Goodin and Philip Pettit. Oxford: Blackwell.

Benjamin, Andrew. 1989. "The Crumbling Narrative: Time, Memory and the Overcoming of Nihilism in 'The Eye of the Scarecrow'". In *The Literate Imagination: Essays on the Novels of Wilson Harris*, ed. Michael Gilkes. London and Basingstoke: Macmillan Caribbean.

Benn, Denis. 2004. *The Caribbean: An Intellectual History 1774–2003*. Kingston: Ian Randle.

Bidima, Jean-Godfrey. 2004. "Philosophy and Literature in Francophone Africa". In *A Companion to African Philosophy*, ed. Kwasi Wiredu. Oxford: Blackwell.

Bilimoria, Purushottama. 1993. "Indian Ethics". In *A Companion to Ethics*, ed. Peter Singer. Oxford: Blackwell.

Billington, Ray. 1997. *Understanding Eastern Philosophy*. London: Routledge.

Blackburn, Simon. 1999. *Think*. New York: Oxford University Press.

Booker, M. Keith, and Dubravka Juraga. 2001. *The Caribbean Novel in English: An Introduction*. Portsmouth: Heinemann.

Boxill, Anthony. 1983. *V.S. Naipaul's Fiction: In Quest of the Enemy*. Fredericton, NB: York Press.

References

Boxill, Bernard R. 2003. "*The Morality of Reparations II*". In *A Companion to African-American Philosophy*, ed. Tommy L. Lott and John P. Pittman. Oxford: Blackwell.

Brathwaite, E. Kamau. 1977. "Houses: A Note on West Indian Literature". *First World* 1, no. 2 (March–April).

Bressler, Charles E. 1994. *Literary Criticism: An Introduction to Theory and Practice.* Englewood Cliffs, NJ: Prentice Hall.

Brodber, Erna. 1988. *Myal.* London: New Beacon.

———. 2003. *The Continent of Black Consciousness: On the History of the African Diaspora from Slavery to the Present Day.* London: New Beacon.

Brontë, Charlotte. 1959. *Jane Eyre.* Introduction and notes by A.C. Ward. London: Longmans.

Campbell, Joseph. 1988. *The Power of Myth.* With Bill Moyers. New York: Anchor.

Camus, Albert. 1955. *The Myth of Sisyphus.* Harmondsworth: Penguin.

Chanter, Tina. 1999. "Irigaray". In *A Companion to Continental Philosophy*, ed. Simon Critchley and William R. Schroeder. Oxford: Blackwell.

———. 2000. "Irigaray, Luce". In *The Concise Routledge Encyclopedia of Philosophy.* London and New York: Routledge.

Chevannes, Barry. 1995. *Rastafari: Roots and Ideology.* Kingston: The Press, University of the West Indies.

Cooke, Michael G. 1990. "The Strains of Apocalypse: Lamming's *Castle* and Brodber's *Jane and Louisa*". *Journal of West Indian Literature* 4, no. 1 (January).

Cooper, David E. 2000. "Existentialist Ethics". In *The Concise Routledge Encyclopedia of Philosophy.* London: Routledge.

Critchley, Simon. 2001. *Continental Philosophy: A Very Short Introduction.* Oxford: Oxford University Press.

Crosby, Donald H. 2000. "Nihilism". In *The Concise Routledge Encyclopedia of Philosophy.* London: Routledge.

Culler, Jonathan. 1997. *Literary Theory: A Very Short Introduction.* Oxford: Oxford University Press.

Davies, David. 2002. "Fiction". In *The Routledge Companion to Aesthetics*, ed. Berys Gaut and Dominic McIver Lopes. London: Routledge.

D'Costa, Jean. 1983. Introduction. *Black Lightning*, by Roger Mais. London: Heinemann.

Diamond, Cora. 1998. "Martha Nussbaum and the Need for Novels". In *Renegotiating Ethics in Literature, Philosophy and Theory*, ed. Jane Adamson et al. Cambridge: Cambridge University Press.

Dostoevsky, Fyodor. 1993. *Notes from Underground.* Trans. Richard Pevear and Larissa Volokhonsky. New York: Vintage Books.

Duff, R.A. 2000. "Responsibility". In *The Concise Routledge Encyclopedia of Philosophy.* London: Routledge.

Durix, Jean-Pierre. 2002. "Origins in *Palace of the Peacock*". In *Theatre of the Arts: Wilson Harris and the Caribbean*, ed. Hena Maës-Jelinek and Bénédicte Ledent. Amsterdam: Rodopi.

Edwards, Paul. 2000. "Suicide, Ethics of". In *The Concise Routledge Encyclopedia of Philosophy*. London: Routledge.

Fanon, Frantz. 1963. *The Wretched of the Earth*. Trans. Constance Farrington. New York: Grove Press.

Feldman, Fred. 1992. *Confrontations with the Reaper: A Philosophical Study of the Nature and Value of Death*. New York: Oxford University Press.

Foucault, Michel. 1970. *The Order of Things*. New York: Vintage Books.

Freire, Paulo. 2003. *Pedagogy of the Oppressed*. Trans. Myrna Benjamin Ramos; intro. Donaldo Macedo. New York: Continuum International.

Gooding, David C. 2000. "Thought Experiments". In *The Concise Routledge Encyclopedia of Philosophy*. London: Routledge.

Gordon, Lewis R., ed. 1997. *Existence in Black*. New York: Routledge.

———. 2000. "The Liberation of Identity". In *A Parliament of Minds*, ed. Michael Tobias et al. Albany: State University of New York Press.

Graham, George. 1993. *Philosophy of Mind: An Introduction*. Oxford: Blackwell.

Greene, Maxine. 1971. "Literature and Human Understanding". In *Aesthetics and Problems of Education*, ed. Ralph A. Smith. Urbana: University of Illinois Press.

———. 1973. *Teacher as Stranger*. Belmont, CA: Wadsworth.

Griffith, Glyne. 1998. "Madness and Counterdiscourse: A Dialogic Encounter between *Wide Sargasso Sea* and *Jane Eyre*". In *The Woman Writer and Caribbean Society*, ed. Helen Pyne-Timothy. Los Angeles: Center for Afro-American Studies Publications, University of California, Los Angeles.

Grimshaw, Jean, and Miranda Fricker. 1996. "Philosophy and Feminism". In *The Blackwell Companion to Philosophy*, ed. Nicholas Bunnin and E.P. Tsui-James. Oxford: Blackwell.

Gutting, Gary. 1994. "Foucault and the History of Madness". In *The Cambridge Companion to Foucault*, ed. Gary Gutting. Cambridge: Cambridge University Press.

Halbfass, Wilhelm. 2000. "Karma and Rebirth, Indian Conceptions of". In *The Concise Routledge Encyclopedia of Philosophy*. London: Routledge.

Hall, Stuart. 2001. "Negotiating Caribbean Identities". In *New Caribbean Thought*, ed. Brian Meeks and Folke Lindhal. Kingston: University of the West Indies Press.

Hamilton, Edith. 1940. *Mythology*. New York: The New American Library.

Hamilton, Sue. 2001. *Indian Philosophy: A Very Short Introduction*. Oxford: Oxford University Press.

Hanfling, Oswald. 1987. *The Quest for Meaning*. Oxford: Blackwell.

Hare, R.M. 1986. "What Is Wrong with Slavery?" In *Applied Ethics*, ed. Peter Singer. Oxford: Oxford University Press.

Harris, Wilson. [1960] 1998. *Palace of the Peacock*. London and Boston: Faber and Faber.

———. 1999. "New Preface to *Palace of the Peacock*". In *Selected Essays of Wilson Harris: The Unfinished Genesis of the Imagination*, ed. Andrew Bundy. London: Routledge.

References

Henderson, Joseph L. 1964. "Ancient Myths and Modern Man". In *Man and His Symbols*, ed. Carl G. Jung. New York: Dell.

Henry, Paget. 1997. "African and Afro-Caribbean Existential Philosophies". In *Existence in Black*, ed. Lewis R. Gordon. New York: Routledge.

——. 2000. *Caliban's Reason: Introducing Afro-Caribbean Philosophy*. New York: Routledge.

Holcomb, Gary, and Kimberly S. Holcomb. 2002. " 'I Made Him': Sadomasochism in Kincaid's *The Autobiography of My Mother*". *Callaloo* 125, no. 3.

Hord, Fred Lee, and Jonathan Scott Lee, eds., 1995. *I Am Because We Are: Readings in Black Philosophy*. Amherst: University of Massachusetts Press.

Irigaray, Luce. 1985. *Speculum of the Other Woman*. Ithaca: Cornell University Press.

James, C.L.R. N.d. *Wilson Harris: A Philosophical Approach.* General Public Lecture Series: West Indian Literature, ed. E.D. Ramesar. St Augustine: Extra-Mural Department, University of the West Indies.

John, Eileen. 2002. "Art and Knowledge". In *The Routledge Companion to Aesthetics*, ed. Berys Gaut and Dominic McIver Lopes. London: Routledge.

Jones, Charles. 1999. *Global Justice: Defending Cosmopolitanism*. Oxford: Oxford University Press.

Kaphagawani, Didier N. 2004. "African Conceptions of a Person". In *A Companion to African Philosophy*, ed. Kwasi Wiredu. Oxford: Blackwell.

Kekes, John. 2000. "Evil". In *The Concise Routledge Encyclopedia of Philosophy*. London: Routledge.

Kieran, Matthew. 2002. "Value of Art". In *The Routledge Companion to Aesthetics*, ed. Berys Gaut and Dominic McIver Lopes. London: Routledge.

Kincaid, Jamaica. 1996. *The Autobiography of My Mother*. Harmondsworth: Plume.

Kotzin, Rhoda Hadassah. 2000. "Ancient Greek Philosophy". In *A Companion to Feminist Philosophy*, ed. Alison M. Jaggar and Iris Marion Young. Oxford: Blackwell.

Kymlicka, Will. 1993. "Community". In *Companion to Contemporary Political Philosophy*, ed. Robert E. Goodin and Philip Pettit. Oxford: Blackwell.

Lamming, George. [1953] 1987. *In the Castle of My Skin*. Harlow: Longman.

——, ed. 1999. *Enterprise of the Indies*. Port of Spain: The Trinidad and Tobago Institute of the West Indies.

Lechte, John. 1994. *Fifty Key Contemporary Thinkers*. London: Routledge.

Lewis, Gordon K. 1983. *Main Currents in Caribbean Thought: The Historical Evolution of Caribbean Society in Its Ideological Aspects*. Kingston: Heinemann.

Lott, Tommy L., and John P. Pittman, eds. 2003. *A Companion to African-American Philosophy*. Oxford: Blackwell.

Lovelace, Earl. 1996. *Salt*. London: Faber and Faber.

Lund, David H. 1999. *Making Sense of It All*. Upper Saddle River, NJ: Prentice Hall.

Mais, Roger. [1955] 1983. *Black Lightning*. London: Heinemann.

Margolis, Joseph. 2000. "The Marriage of History and Culture". In *A Parliament of Minds*, ed. Michael Tobias et al. Albany: State University of New York Press.

Marshall, Paule. 1969. *The Chosen Place, the Timeless People*. London: Longman.

Masolo, D.A. 2004. "Western and African Communitarianism: A Comparison". In *A Companion to African Philosophy*, ed. Kwasi Wiredu. Oxford: Blackwell.

Mbiti, John S. 1969. *African Religions and Philosophies*. New York: Anchor.

McGinn, Colin. 1997. *Ethics, Evil and Fiction*. Oxford: Clarendon Press.

Meek, Sandra. 2000–2001. " 'The Penitential Island': The Question of Liberation in Earl Lovelace's *Salt*". *Journal of Caribbean Studies* 15, no. 3 (Winter–Spring).

Mehta, Brinda. 2004. *Diasporic (Dis)locations: Indo-Caribbean Women Writers Negotiate the Kala Pani*. Kingston: University of the West Indies Press.

Menkiti, Ifeanya A. 2004. "On the Normative Conception of a Person". In *A Companion to African Philosophy*, ed. Kwasi Wiredu. Oxford: Blackwell.

Mills, Charles. 1997a. *The Racial Contract*. Ithaca: Cornell University Press.

———. 1997b. "Smadditizin". *Caribbean Quarterly* 43, no. 2.

Mohanty, J.N. 1993. *Essays on Indian Philosophy*. ed. P. Bilimoria. Oxford: Oxford University Press.

Mordecai, Pamela, and Betty Wilson, eds. 1989. *Her True-True Name: An Anthology of Women's Writing from the Caribbean*. Oxford: Heinemann.

Morris, Kathryn E. 2002. "Jamaica Kincaid's Voracious Bodies: Engendering a Carib(bean) Woman". *Callaloo* 25, no. 3.

Murdoch, Iris. 1992. *Metaphysics as a Guide to Morals*. Harmondsworth: Penguin.

Nagel, Thomas. 1987. *What Does It All Mean?* Oxford: Oxford University Press.

Naipaul, V.S. [1961] 1969. *A House for Mr Biswas*. Harmondsworth: Penguin.

———. 1984. *Finding the Centre*. New York: Vintage.

Neander, Karen. 2000. "Mental Illness, Concept of". In *The Concise Routledge Encyclopedia of Philosophy*. London: Routledge.

Neill, Alex. 2002. "Tragedy". In *The Routledge Companion to Aesthetics*, ed. Berys Gaut and Dominic McIver Lopes. London: Routledge.

Novitz, David. 1993. "Fiction and the Growth of Knowledge". In *Contemporary Philosophy of Art*, ed. John W. Bender and H. Gene Blocker. Englewood Cliffs, NJ: Prentice Hall.

Nussbaum, Martha. 1990. *Love's Knowledge: Essays on Philosophy and Literature*. New York: Oxford University Press.

Oaklander, L. Nathan. 1992. *Existentialist Philosophy: An Introduction*. Englewood Cliffs, NJ: Prentice Hall.

O'Callaghan, Evelyn. 1996. "The Outsider's Voice: White Creole Women Novelists in the Caribbean Literary Tradition". In *The Routledge Reader in Caribbean Literature*, ed. Alison Donnell and Sarah Lawson Welsh. London: Routledge.

———. 1998. "Engineering the Female Subject: Erna Boodber's *Myal*". In *The Woman Writer and Caribbean Society*, ed. Helen Pyne-Timothy. Los Angeles: Center for Afro-American Studies Publications, University of California, Los Angeles.

Parker, David. 1998. "Introduction: The Turn to Ethics in the 1990s." In *Renegotiating Ethics in Literature, Philosophy and Theory*, ed. Jane Adamson et al. Cambridge: Cambridge University Press.

Patterson, H. Orlando. 1964. *The Children of Sisyphus*. Kingston: Bolivar Press.

———. 2001. *Freedom*. Vol. 1: *Freedom in the Making of Western Culture*. New York: Basic Books.

———. 2004. "Ecumenical America, Global Culture and the American Cosmos". In *The Birth of Caribbean Civilisation: A Century of Ideas about Culture and Identity, Nation and Society*, ed. O. Nigel Bolland. Kingston: Ian Randle.

Persaud, Lakshmi. 1993. *Sastra*. Leeds: Peepal Tree.

Phillips, Stephen H. 1999. "The Self and Person in Indian Philosophy". In *A Companion to World Philosophies*, ed. Eliot Deutsch and Ron Bontekoe. Oxford: Blackwell.

Priest, Stephen, ed., 2001. *Jean-Paul Sartre: Basic Writings*. London: Routledge.

Proulx, Annie. 1999. *Close Range: Wyoming Stories*. New York: Simon and Schuster.

Putnam, Hilary. 1993. "Literature, Science and Reflection". In *Contemporary Philosophy of Art*, ed. John W. Bender and H. Gene Blocker. Englewood Cliffs, NJ: Prentice Hall.

Rahim, Jennifer. 1999. "The 'Limbo Imagination' and New World Reformation in Earl Lovelace's *Salt*". *Small Axe*, no. 5 (March).

Ramchand, Kenneth. 2004. *The West Indian Novel and Its Background*. Kingston: Ian Randle.

Rhys, Jean. [1966] 1997. *Wide Sargasso Sea*. Harmondsworth: Penguin.

Rickman, H.P. 1996. *Philosophy in Literature*. Madison: Fairleigh Dickinson University Press.

Rinpoche, Sogyal. 1992. *The Tibetan Book of Living and Dying*. London: Rider.

Rohlehr, Gordon. 1977. "Character and Reflection in *A House for Mr. Biswas*". In *Critical Perspectives on V.S. Naipaul*, ed. Robert D. Hamner. Washington, DC: Three Continents Press.

Ruckmani, T.S. 2000. "Indian Theories of the Self". In *The Concise Routledge Encyclopedia of Philosophy*. London: Routledge.

Salick, Roydon. 1986. "The East Indian Female in Three West Indian Novels of Adolescence". *Caribbean Quarterly* 32, nos. 1 and 2.

Sartre, Jean-Paul. 1966. *Being and Nothingness*. New York: Washington Square Press.

Satchell, Veront M. 2000. "Reparation and Emancipation". Churches Emancipation Lecture. Webster Memorial United Church, Church of St Mary the Virgin and Bethel Baptist Church, Kingston, Jamaica.

Schuler, Monica. 1979. "Myalism and the African Religious Tradition in Jamaica". In *Africa and the Caribbean: The Legacies of a Link*, ed. Margaret E. Crahan and Franklin W. Knight. Baltimore: Johns Hopkins University Press.

Scruton, Roger. 1996. *A Dictionary of Political Thought*. 2nd ed. London: Macmillan.

Senior, Olive. 2003. *Encyclopedia of Jamaican Heritage*. Red Hills, Jamaica: Twin Guinep.

Serequeberhan, Tsenay, ed. 1991. *African Philosophy: The Essential Readings*. New York: Paragon House.

Shapiro, Ian. 2000. "Human Nature". In *The Concise Routledge Encyclopedia of Philosophy*. London: Routledge.

Simmons, Diane. 1994. *Jamaica Kincaid*. New York: Twayne.

Singer, Peter. 1981. *The Expanding Circle: Ethics and Sociobiology*. New York: New American Library.

Solomon, Robert C. 1982. *The Big Questions*. New York: Harcourt Brace College Publishers.

Sophocles. 1965. "Oedipus the King". In *Greek Drama*, ed. Moses Hadas. New York: Bantam Books.

Spivak, Gayatri Chakraworty. 1995. "Three Women's Texts and a Critique of Imperialism". In *The Post-colonial Studies Reader*, ed. Bill Ashcroft, Gareth Griffiths, and Helen Tiffin. London: Routledge.

Sprintzer, David A. 2000. "Camus, Albert". In *The Concise Routledge Encyclopedia of Philosophy*. London: Routledge.

Stevenson, Leslie. 1974. *Seven Theories of Human Nature*. New York: Oxford University Press.

Szasz, Thomas S. 1975. "The Myth of Mental Illness". In *Ethics in Perspective: A Reader*, ed. Karsten J. Struhl and Paula Rothenberg Struhl. New York: Random House.

Tussman, Joseph. 1977. *Government and the Mind*. Oxford: Oxford University Press.

Vanterpool, Rudolph. 2003. "Subsistence Welfare Benefits as Property Interests: Legal Theories and Moral Considerations". In *A Companion to African-American Philosophy*, ed. Tommy L. Lott and John P. Pittman. Oxford: Blackwell.

Warner-Lewis, Maureen. 2003. *Central Africa in the Caribbean: Transcending Time, Transforming Cultures*. Kingston: University of the West Indies Press.

Warnock, Mary. 1970. *Existentialism*. Oxford: Oxford University Press.

Wilkins, Nadine. 1988. "The Medical Profession in Jamaica in the Post-emancipation Period". *Jamaica Journal* 21, no. 4.

Williams, Paul. 2000. "Buddhist Concept of Emptiness". In *The Concise Routledge Encyclopedia of Philosophy*. London: Routledge.

Wiredu, Kwasi, ed. 2004. *A Companion to African Philosophy*. Oxford: Blackwell.

Woods, Julian F. 2000. "Fatalism, Indian". In *The Concise Routledge Encyclopedia of Philosophy*. London: Routledge.

Yun, Lisa Li-Shen. 2004. "An Afro-Chinese Caribbean: Cultural Cartographies of Contrariness in the Work of Antonio Chuffat Latour, Margaret Cezair-Thompson, and Patricia Powell". *Caribbean Quarterly* 50, no. 2.

Zack, Naomi. 1993. *Race and Mixed Race*. Philadelphia: Temple University Press.

Zemach, Eddy M. 1995. "Truth in Art". In *A Companion to Aesthetics*, ed. David Cooper. Oxford: Blackwell.

Index

French Revolution, 83, 101
friendship, role of in meaningful life,
19–21

Gandhi, M.K., *Satyagraha*, 70
Garvey, Marcus, "back to Africa" movement,
15
gender relations, in *Wide Sargasso Sea*,
56–72, 125
Gordon, Lewis, 44–45, 48, 53
Greene, Maxine, 34, 35, 42, 81
Griffith, Glyne, 56
Gutting, Gary, 60

Haitian Revolution, 101
Halbfass, Wilhelm, 89
Hall, Stuart, 123
Hamilton, Edith, 46, 87–88
Hamilton, Sue, 28
Hare, R.M., 101
Harris, Wilson, *Palace of the Peacock*, 26–32,
124
Havel, Vaclav, 109–10
Heart of Darkness (Conrad), 27
Hegel, G.W.F., 1, 16, 26, 68, 83
Heidegger, Martin, 26
Henry, Paget, 26, 47, 50
hermeneutics, 4
Hinduism
concept of the self, 28–29, 30, 31
fatalism in, 35–36
karma, and rebirth, 87–89
historical subordination
and process of smadditization, 41–42
of women, 56–72
historicism
in Afro-Caribbean philosophy, 6
as awareness of the human condition,
12–13, 14
and historical change, 15–16
Homer, *Odyssey*, 27
humanism, 101, 127
human understanding, and human nature,
34–35, 41
Hume, David, 94

Husserl, Edmund, 4

illfare, 78
Indian philosophical tradition, 87–89. *See
also* Buddhism; Hinduism
Indians, West Indian migration of,
89–90
inner nature, spiritual world of, 47, 50
In the Castle of My Skin (Lamming), 6–16,
104, 122–23
historicism in, 12–13, 14
Irigaray, Luce, 116, 119
feminist critique of Allegory of the
Cave, 112–13, 121, 127
Speculum of the Other Woman, 112

Jainism, karma, and rebirth, 87–88
Jamaican folklore
duppies, 48
Sisyphean cycle in, 49–50
suspicion of sculpture in, 22
James, C.L.R., 26
Jane Eyre (Brontë), as counterdiscourse to
Wide Sargasso Sea, 56–72
Jones, Charles, 96
journey motif, in quest myths, 27–28, 29
Juraga, Dubravka, 32, 54
justice, principle of, 127
in reparations debate, 100–101

Kant, Immanuel, 1, 24, 33
Kaphagawani, Didier N., 74, 75, 77
karma, 87–97
creolization of in West Indies, 89
and cultural conflict, 96–97
and free will, 90–95, 126
types of, 88
Kincaid, Jamaica
Autobiography of my Mother, The,
111–21, 127
voicing of female subjectivity, 121
knowledge
by acquaintance, 114–16
conceptual knowledge, 34, 36–39, 124
empathetic knowledge, 34–35, 39–41, 124

Index

LaVergne, TN USA
10 March 2010
175570LV00004B/30/P